Back to the Roots

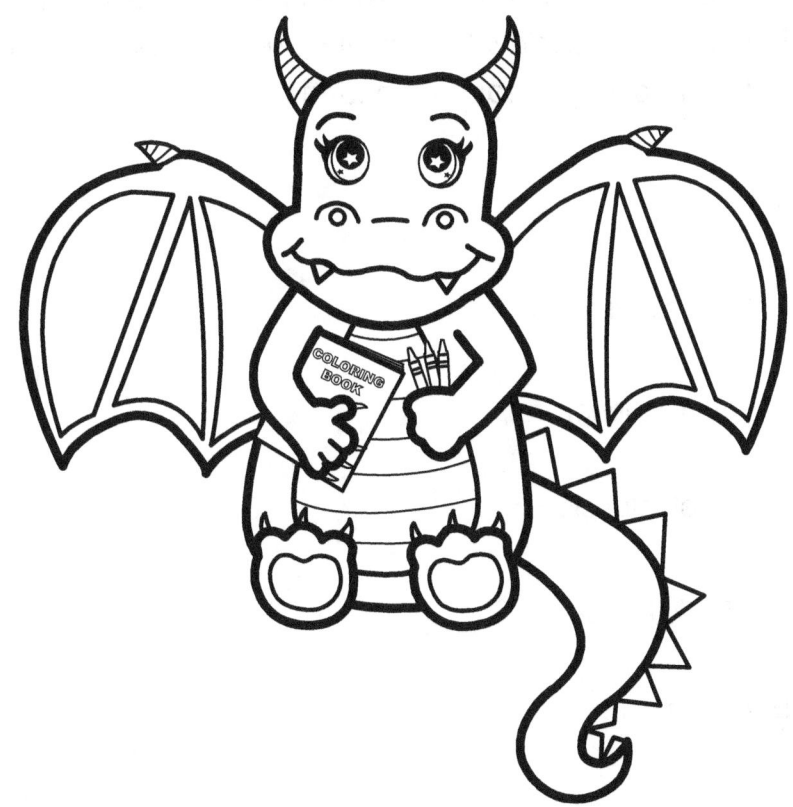

A collect of coloring pages from the very best of Roots of Design.

Jeanette Wummel

Coloring Tip:

When coloring with markers place a piece of paper between pages to prevent bleeding to your next design.

Acknowledgments

Thank you for all your support! Because of people like you, you make me want to continue to create art for the world. You are awesome! I would like to give a special thank you to Jessica Julia McDonald who help inspired the name of this book and to my Coloring Roots Group on Facebook for all the ideas.

Follow me

Facebook:
www.facebook.com/TheRootsofDesign

Facebook Group:
www.facebook.com/group/ColoringRoots

Instagram:
www.instagram.com/therootsofdesign

Twitter:
https://twitter.com/Roots_Of_Design

Etsy:
www.RootsDesign.Etsy.com

Website/Blog:
www.TheRootsofDesign.com

Copyright

Copyright © 2019 by Jeanette Wummel and The Roots of Design

All rights reserved. Designs are intended for personal use. No part of this book may be reproduced or transmitted in any form or by any means, electronic or mechanical, without written permission from the publisher.

Published and Manufactured in the United States
www.TheRootsOfDesign.com

Designs: Jeanette Wummel

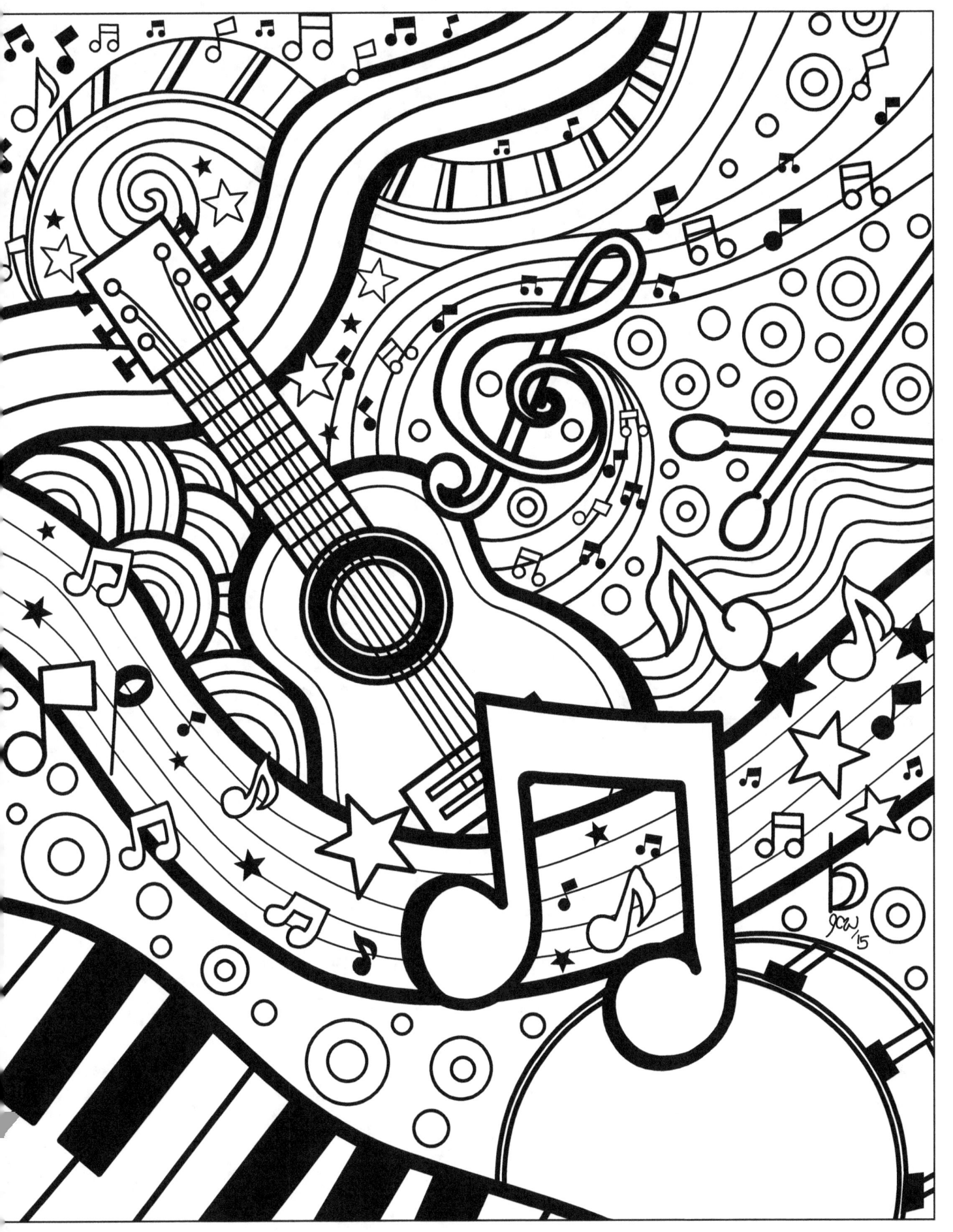

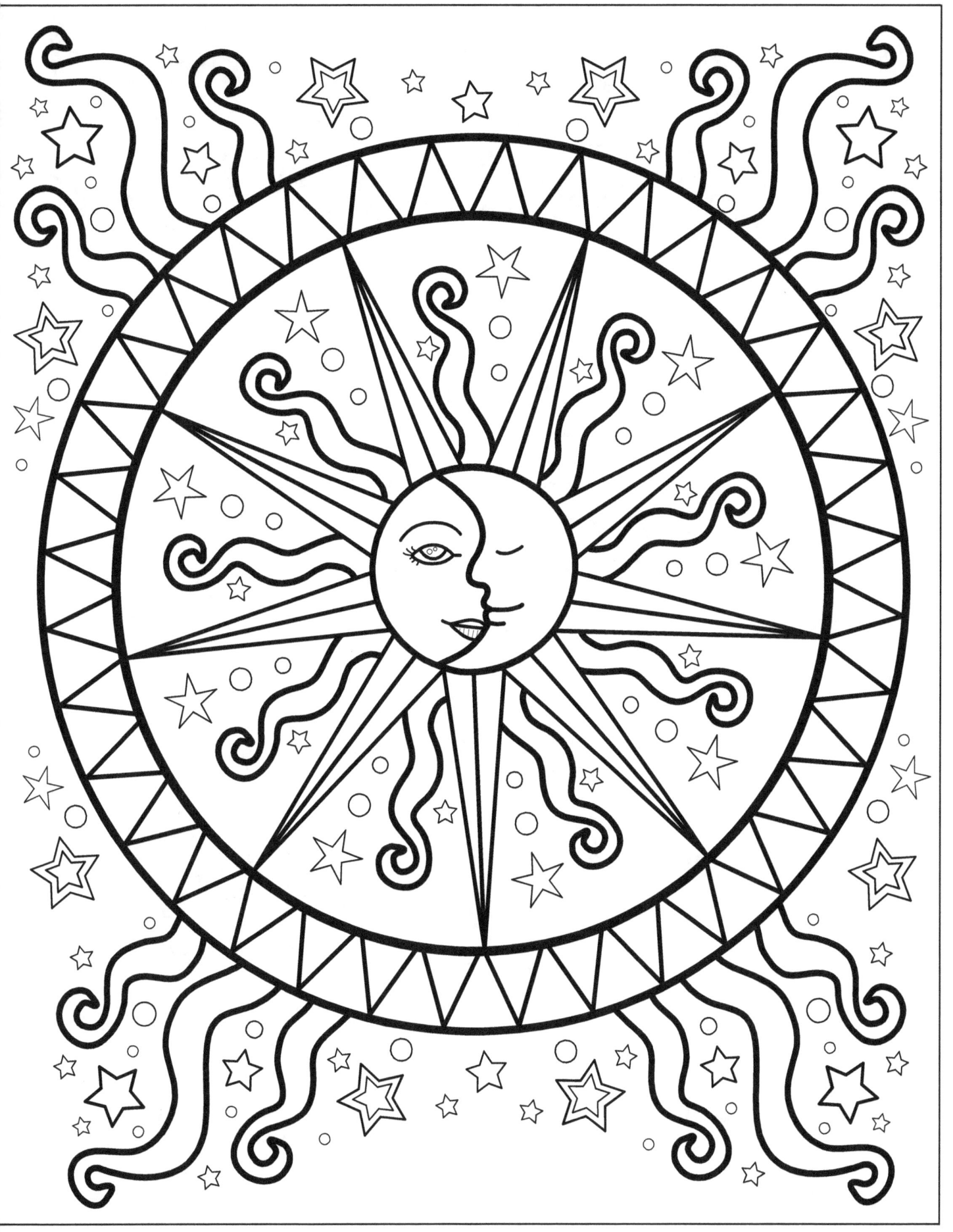

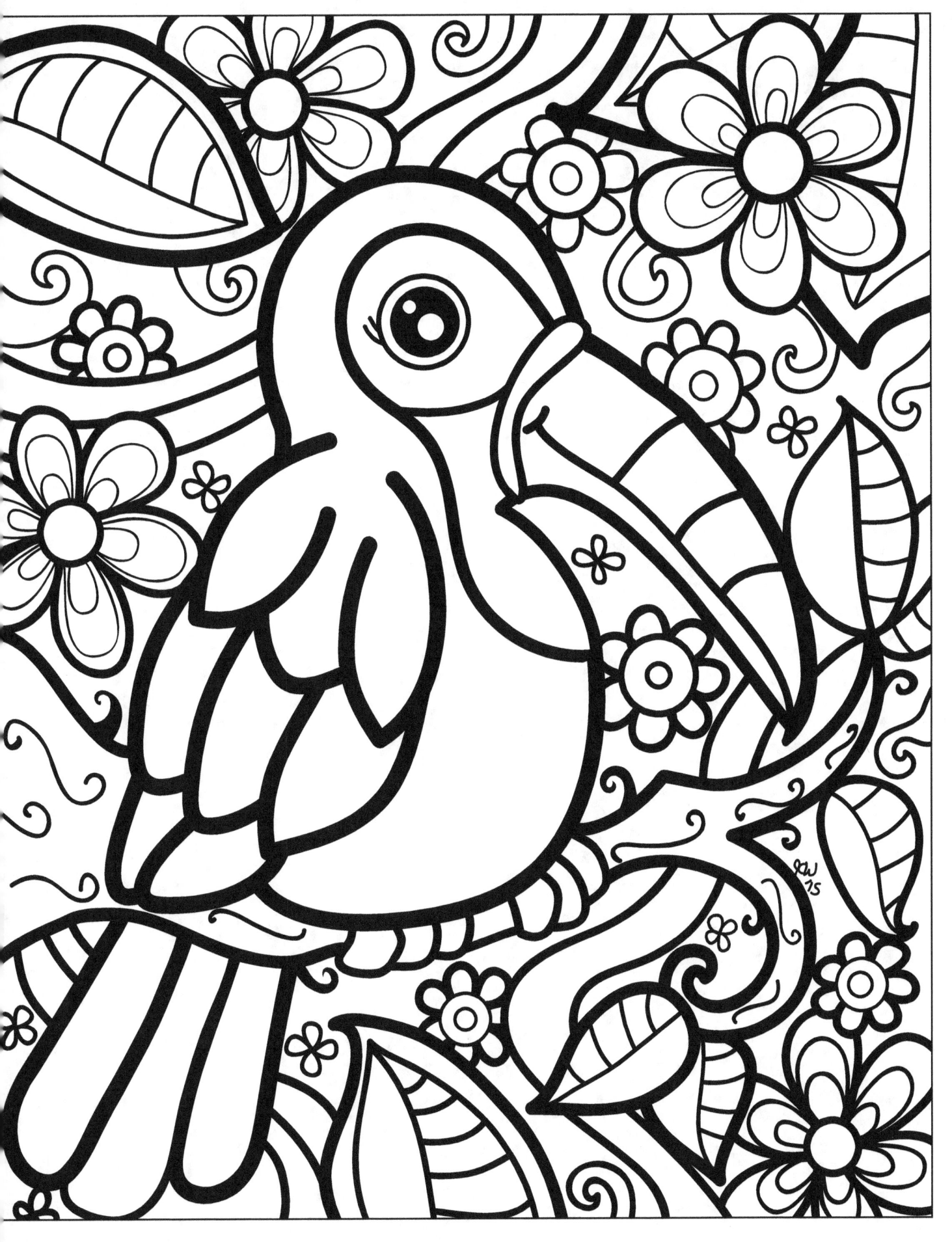

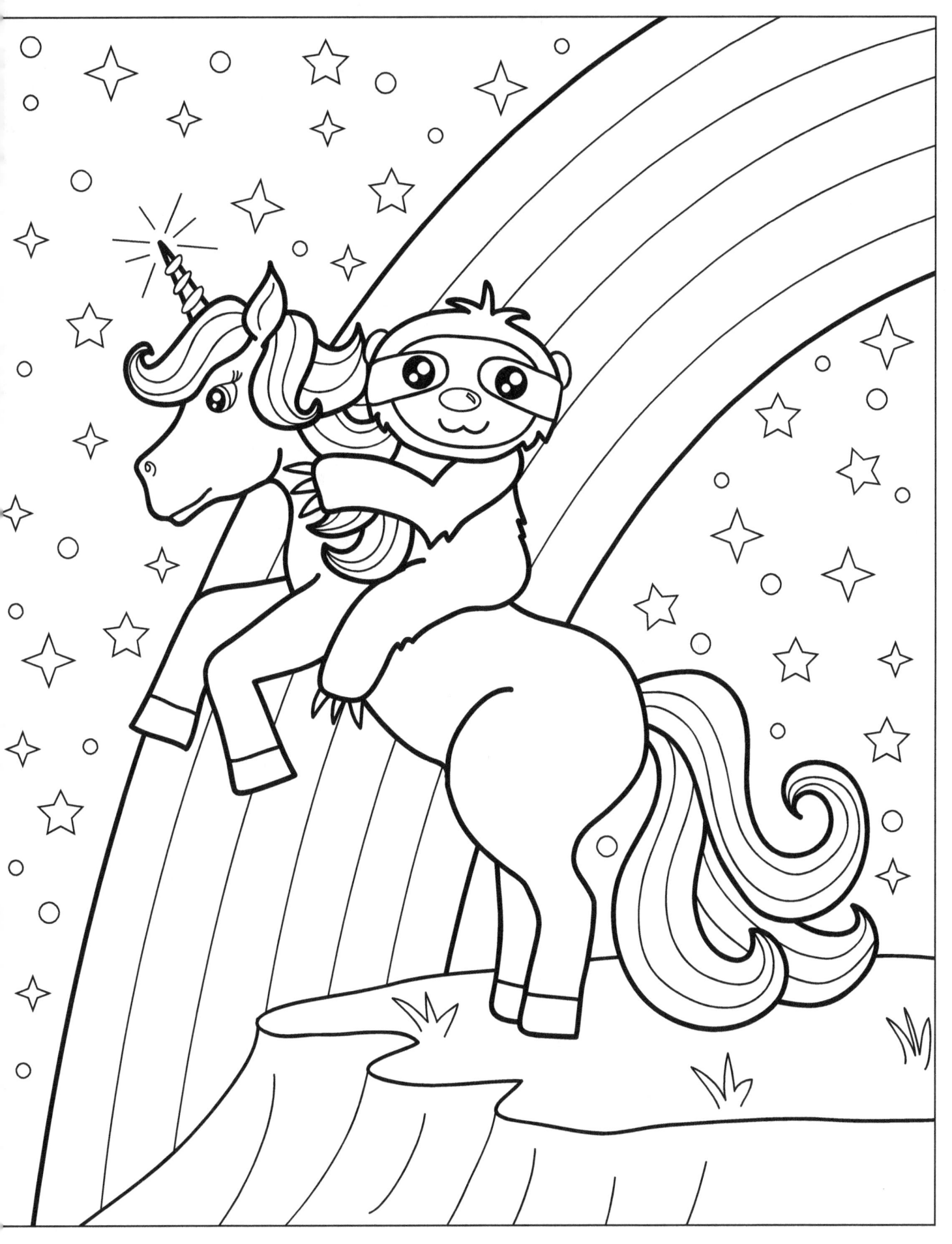

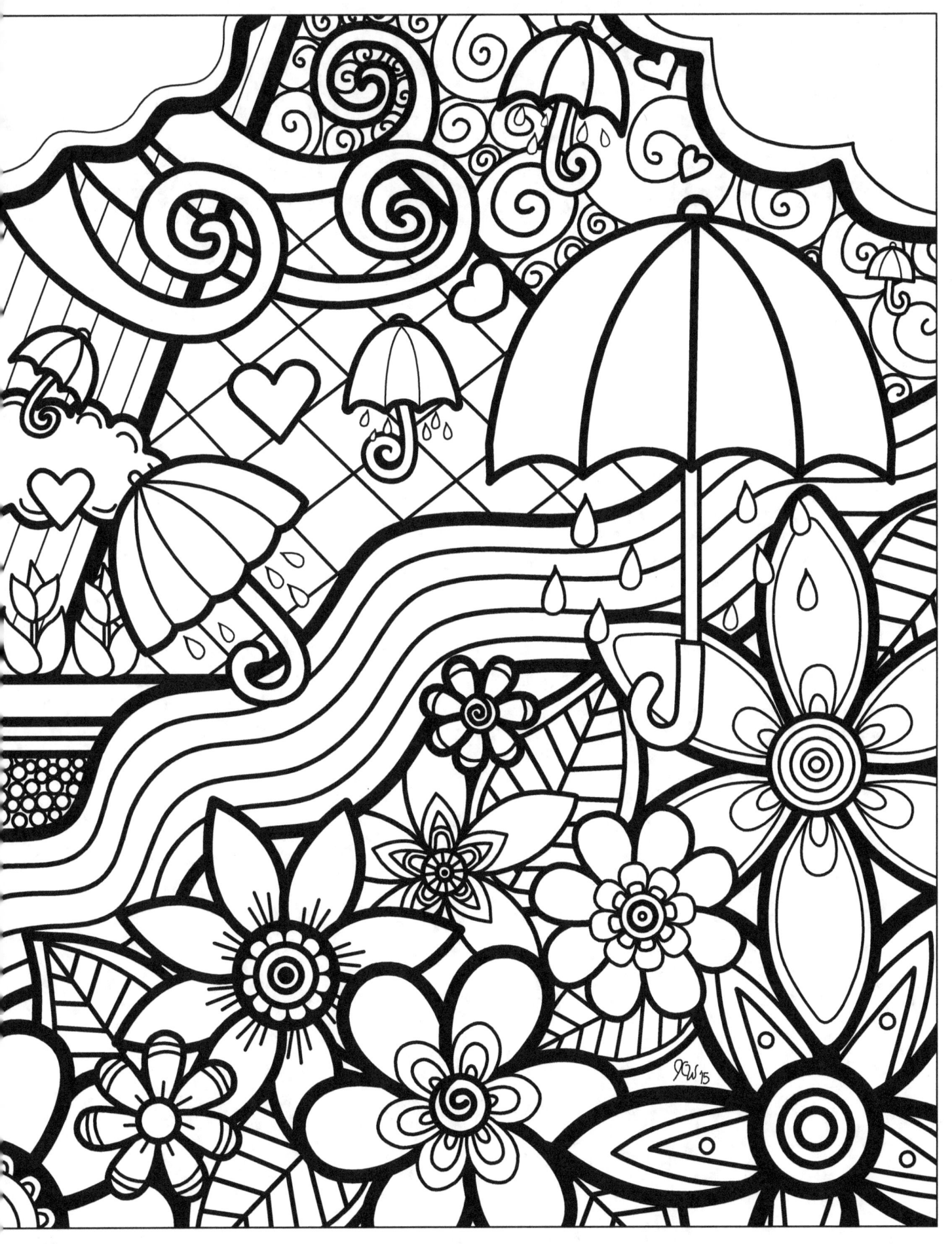

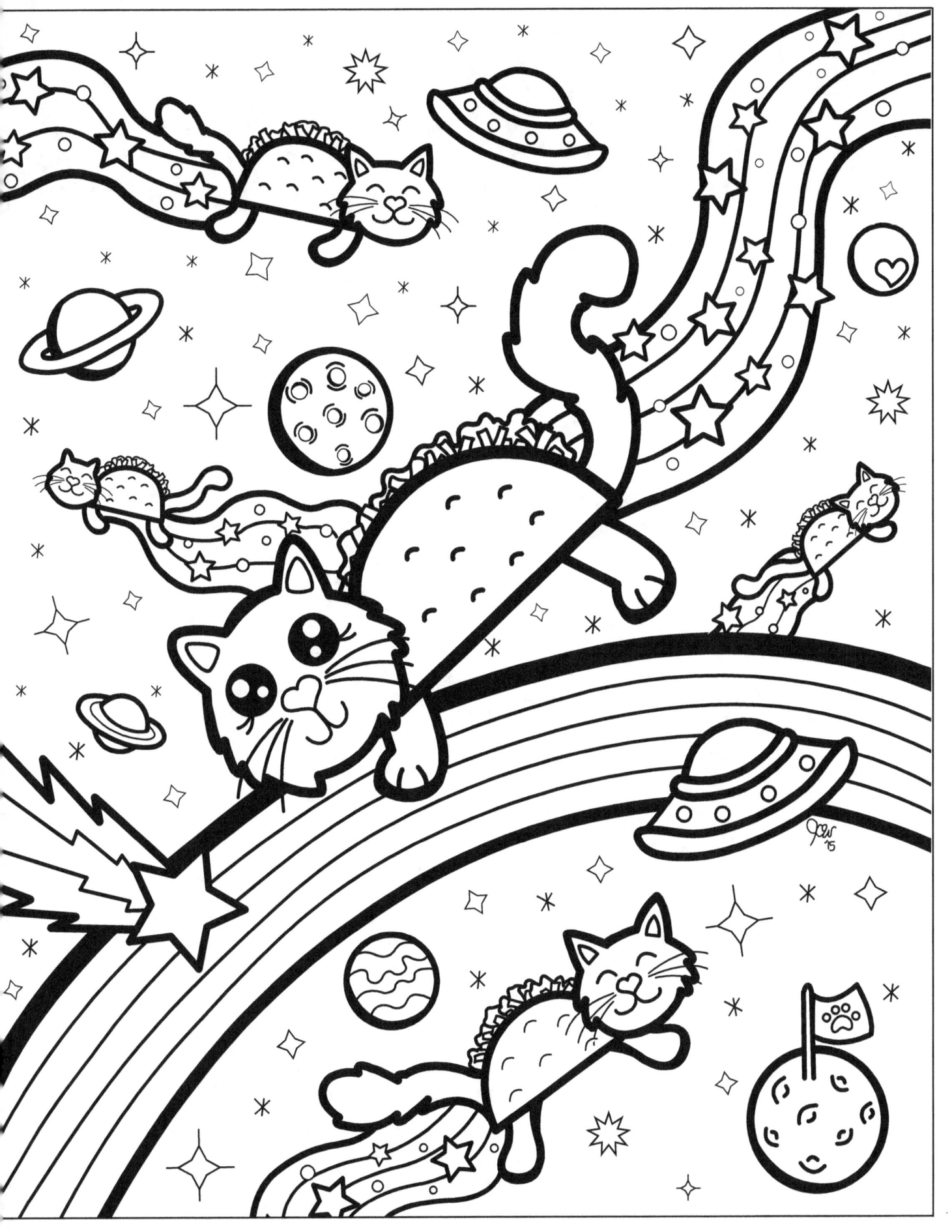

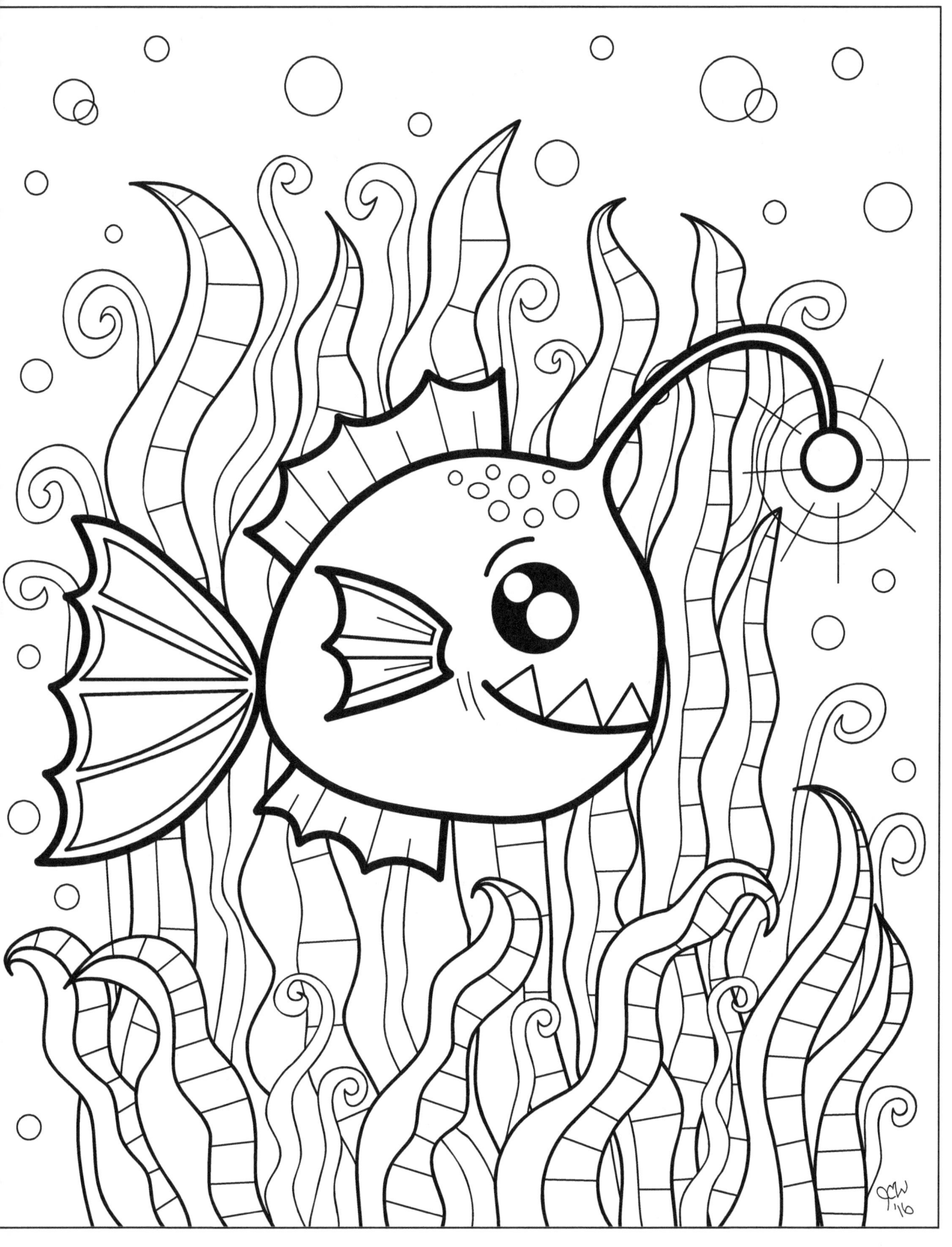

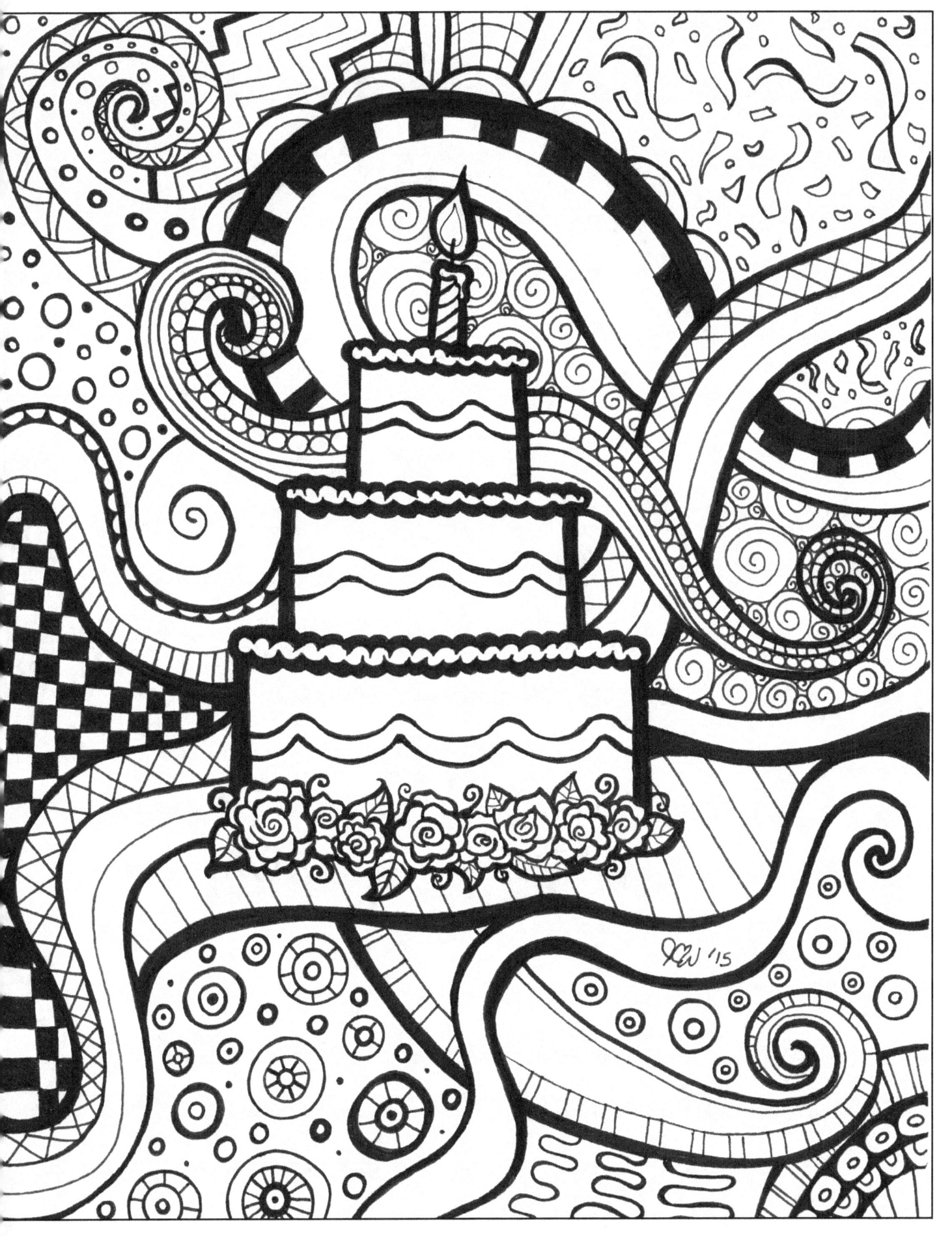

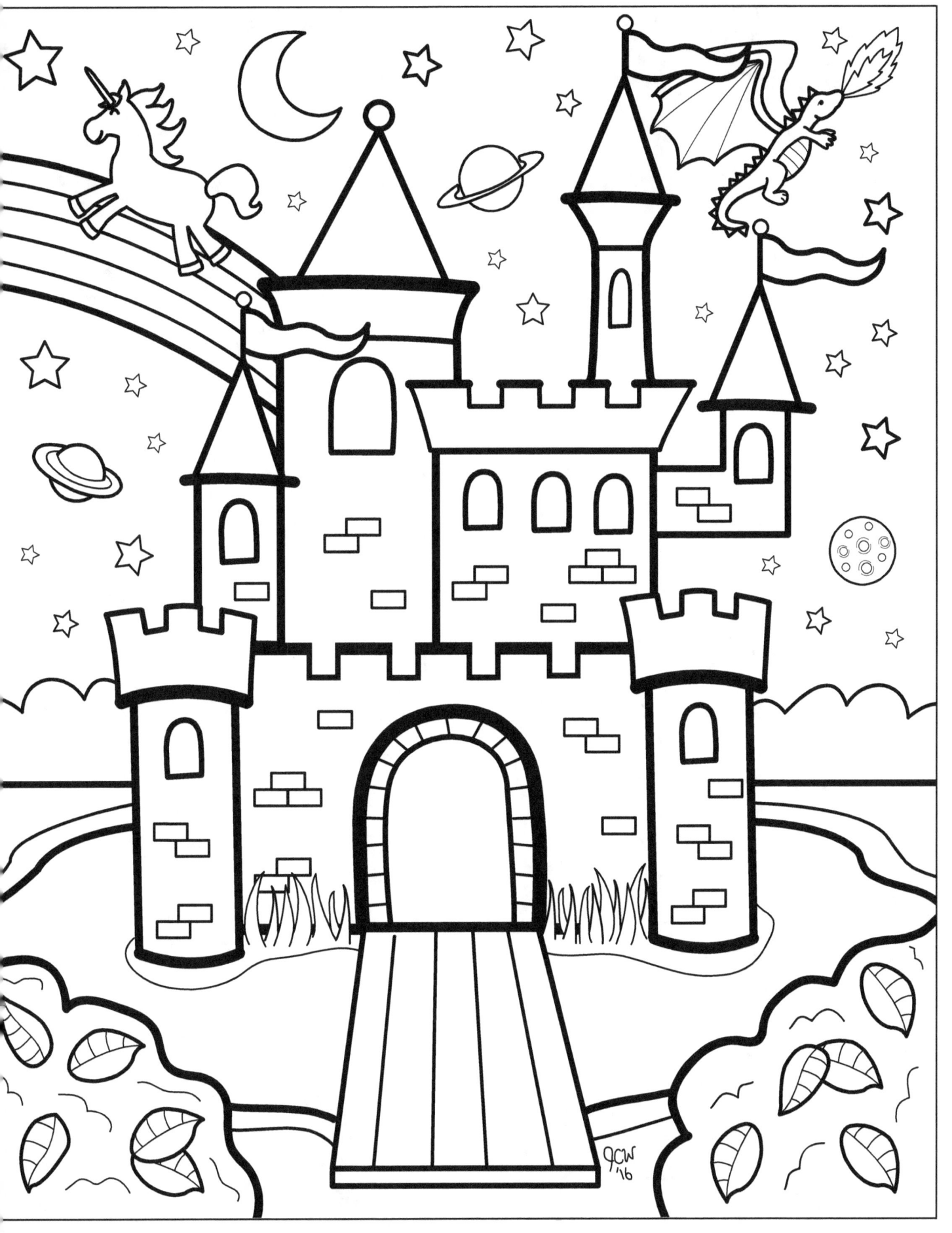

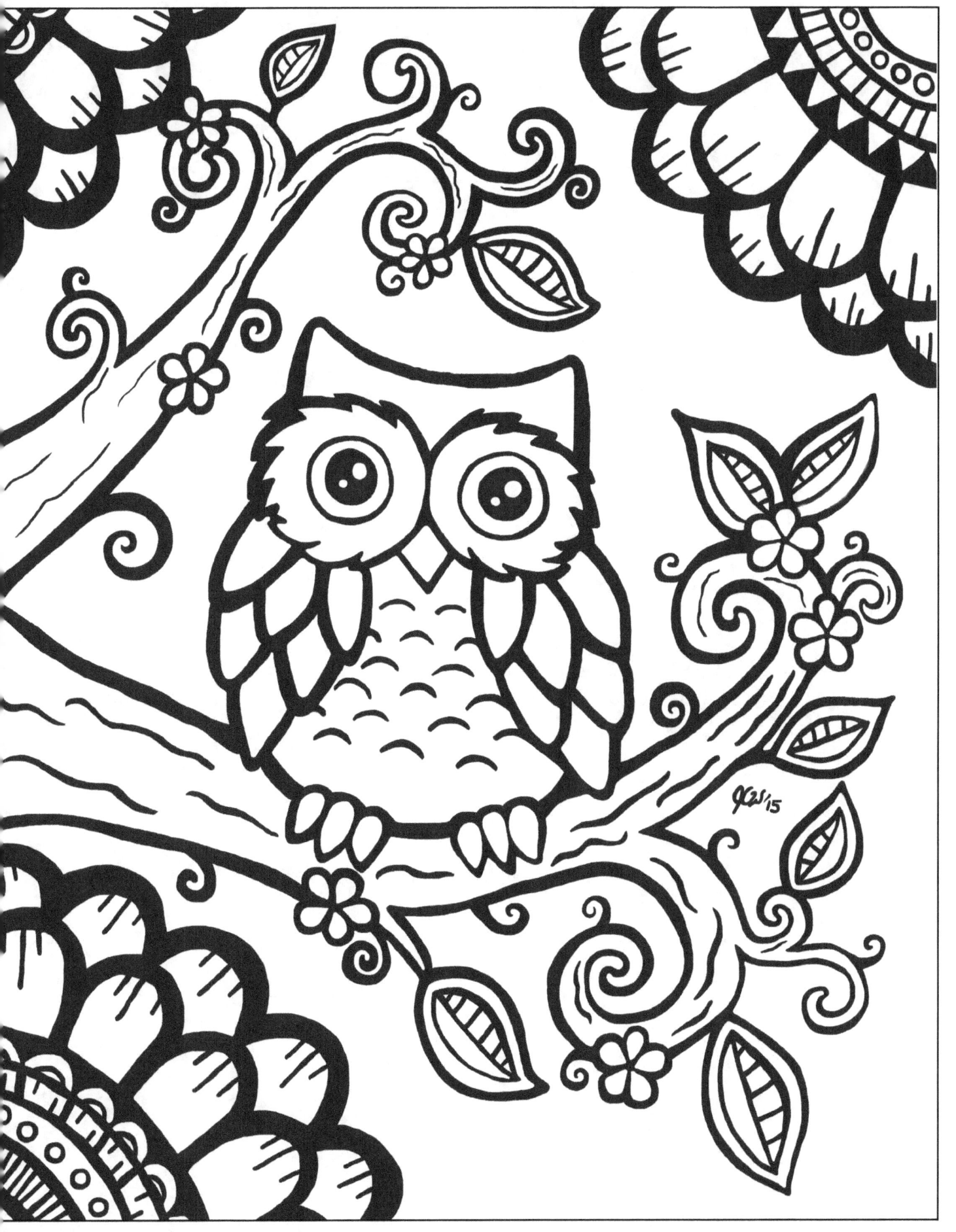

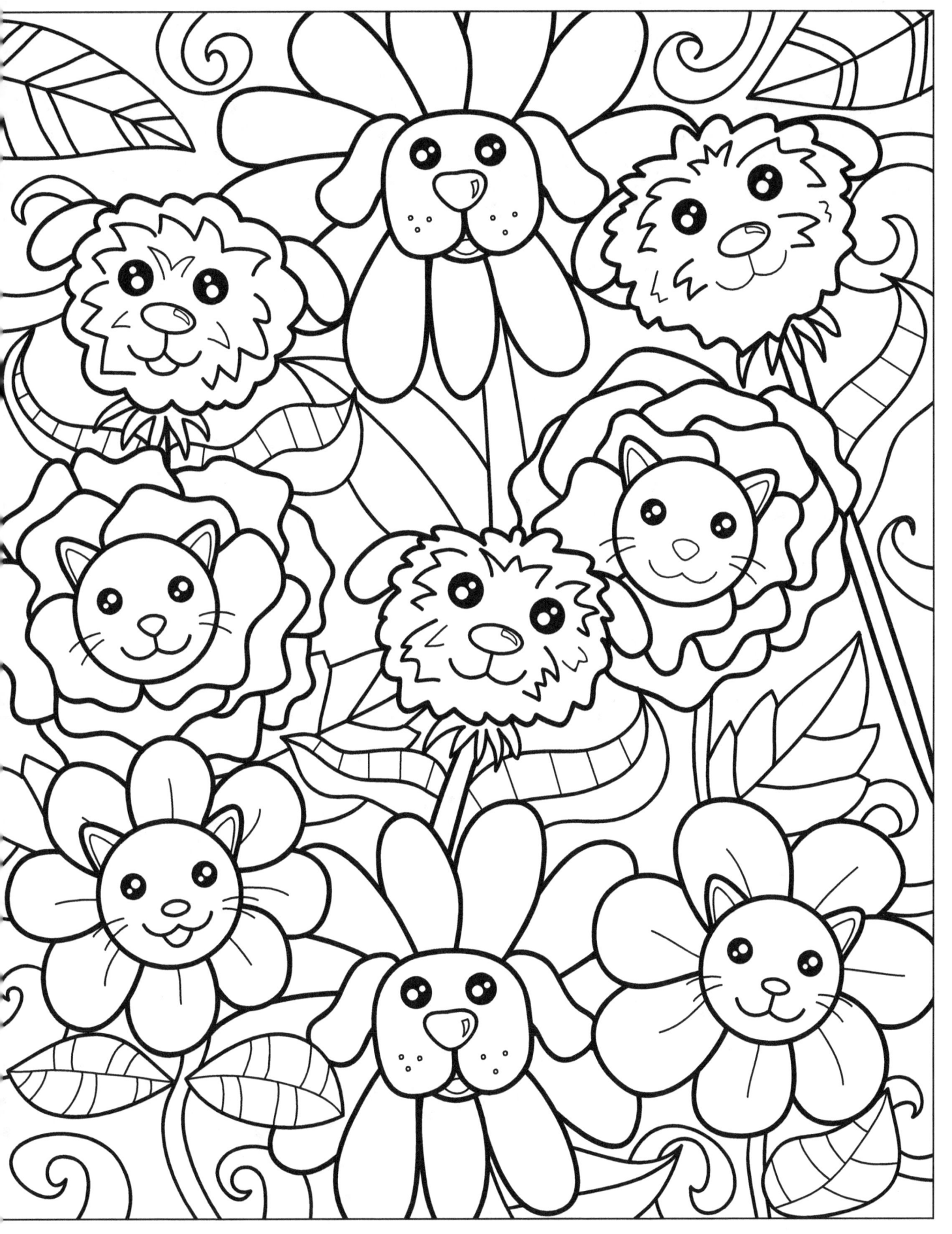

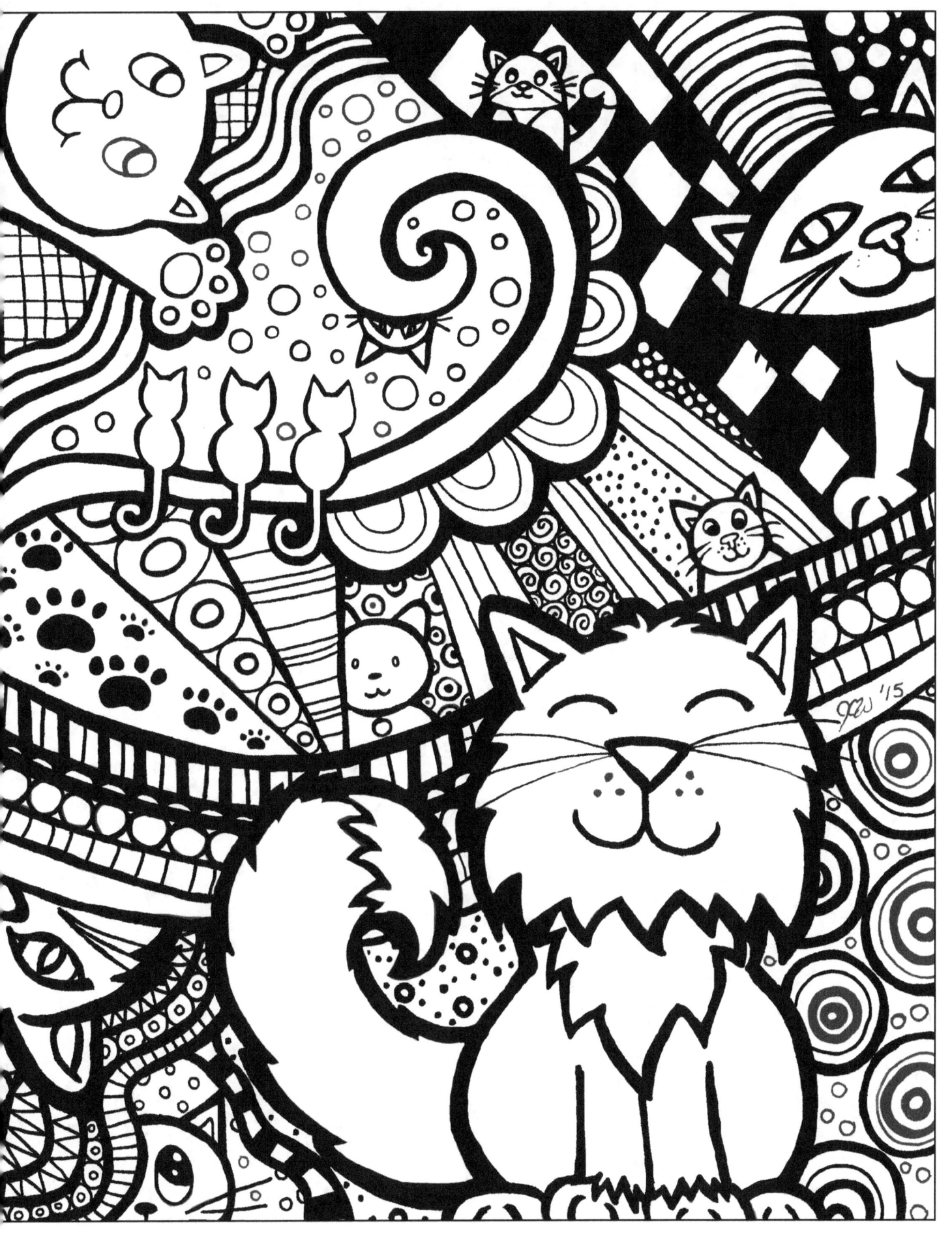

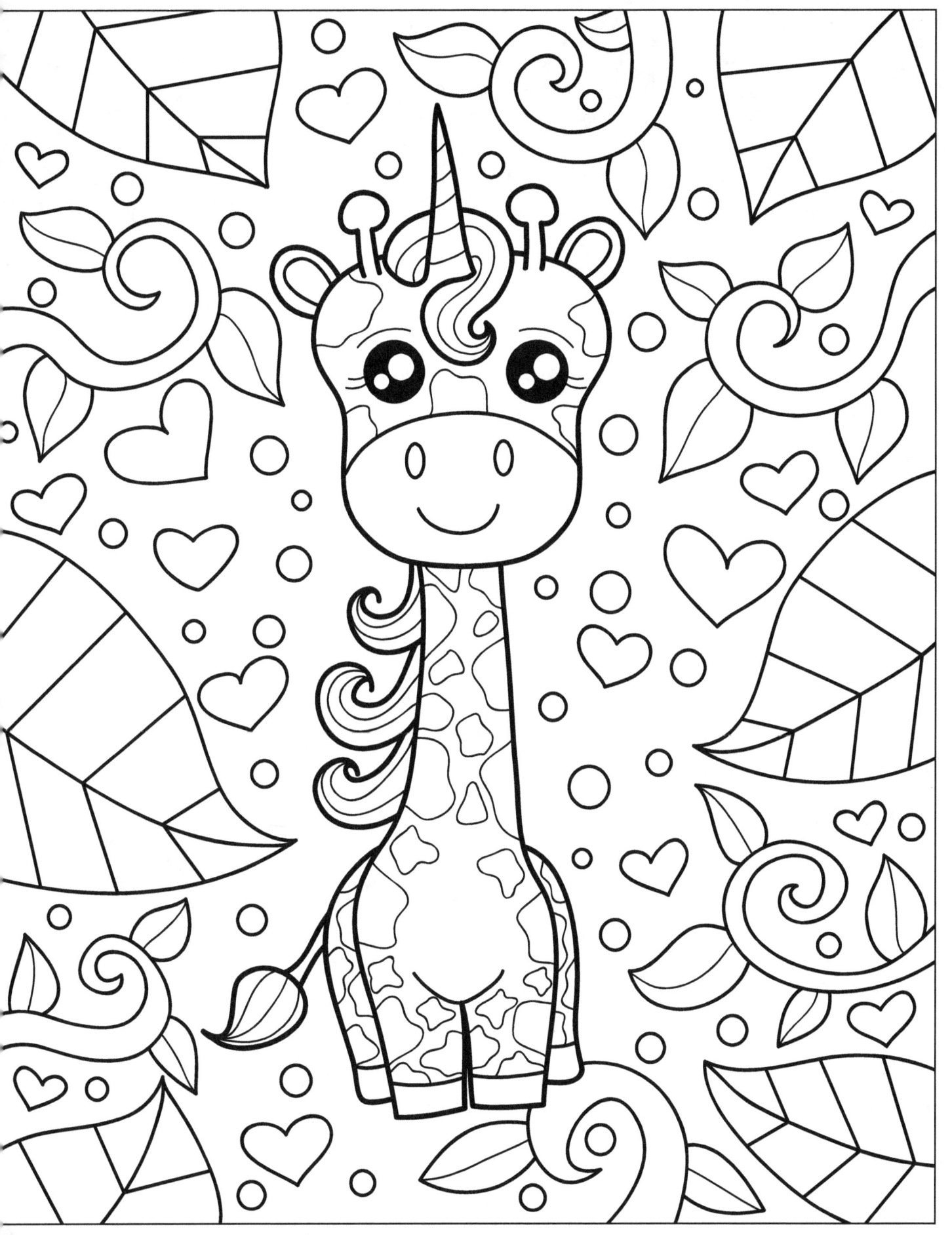

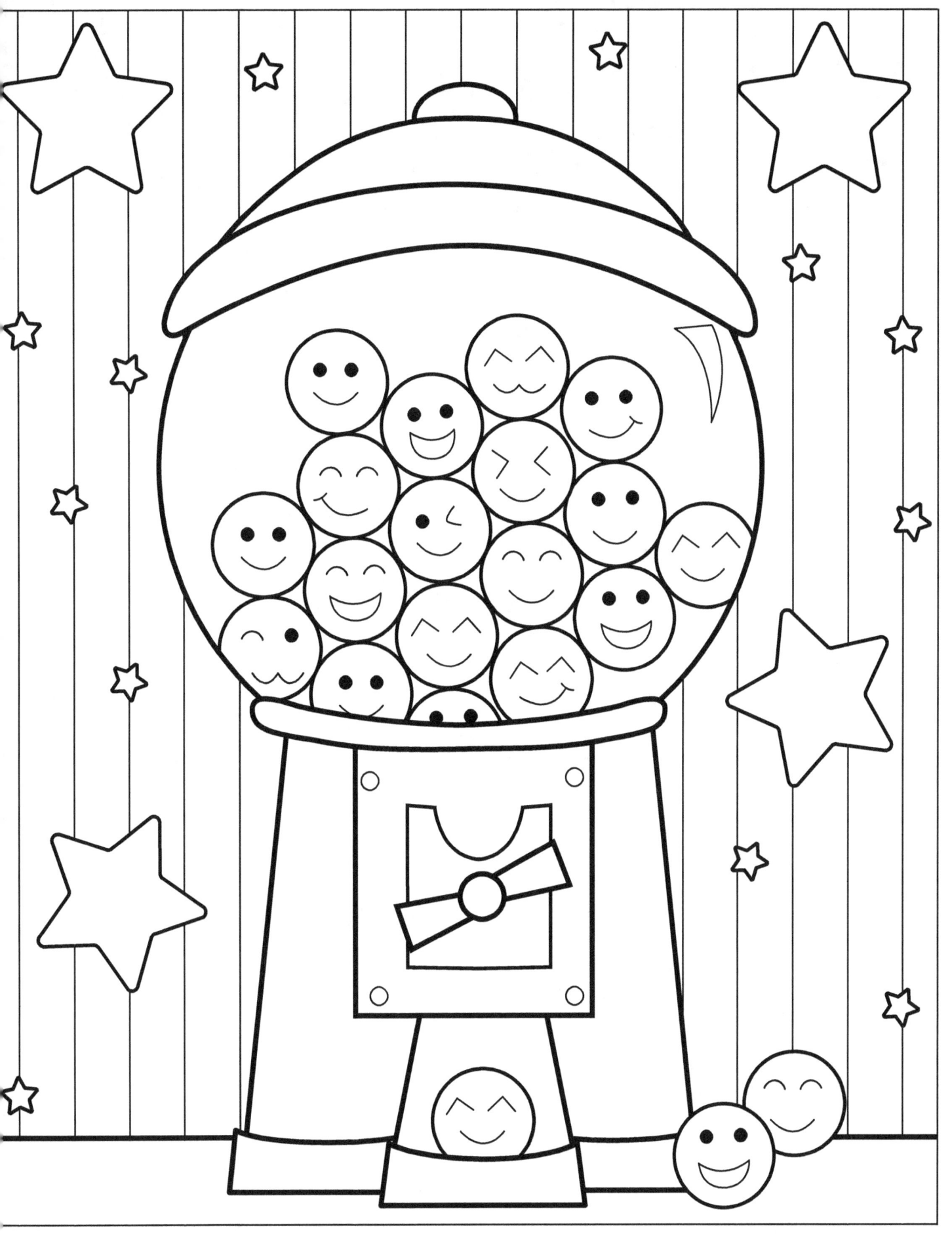

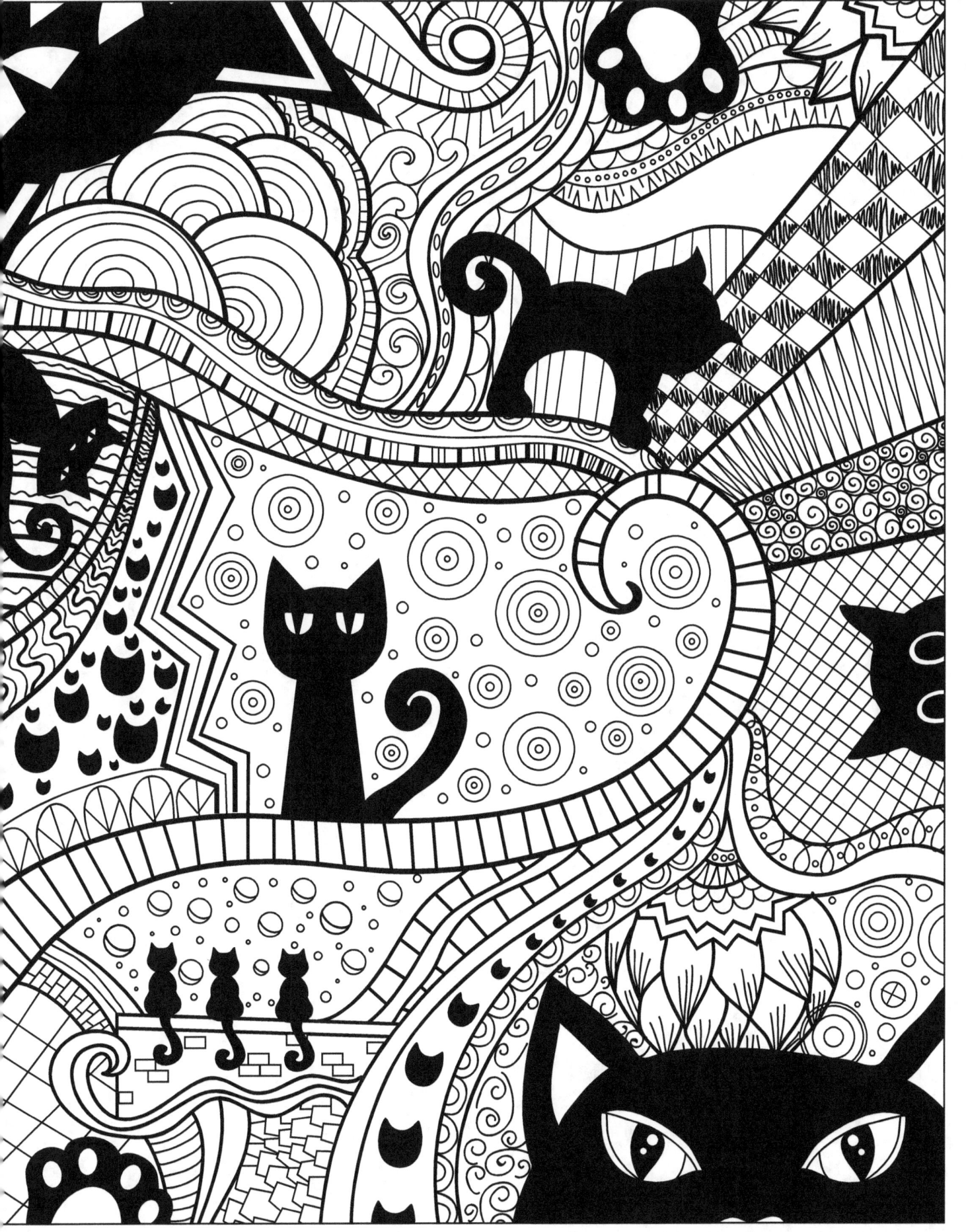

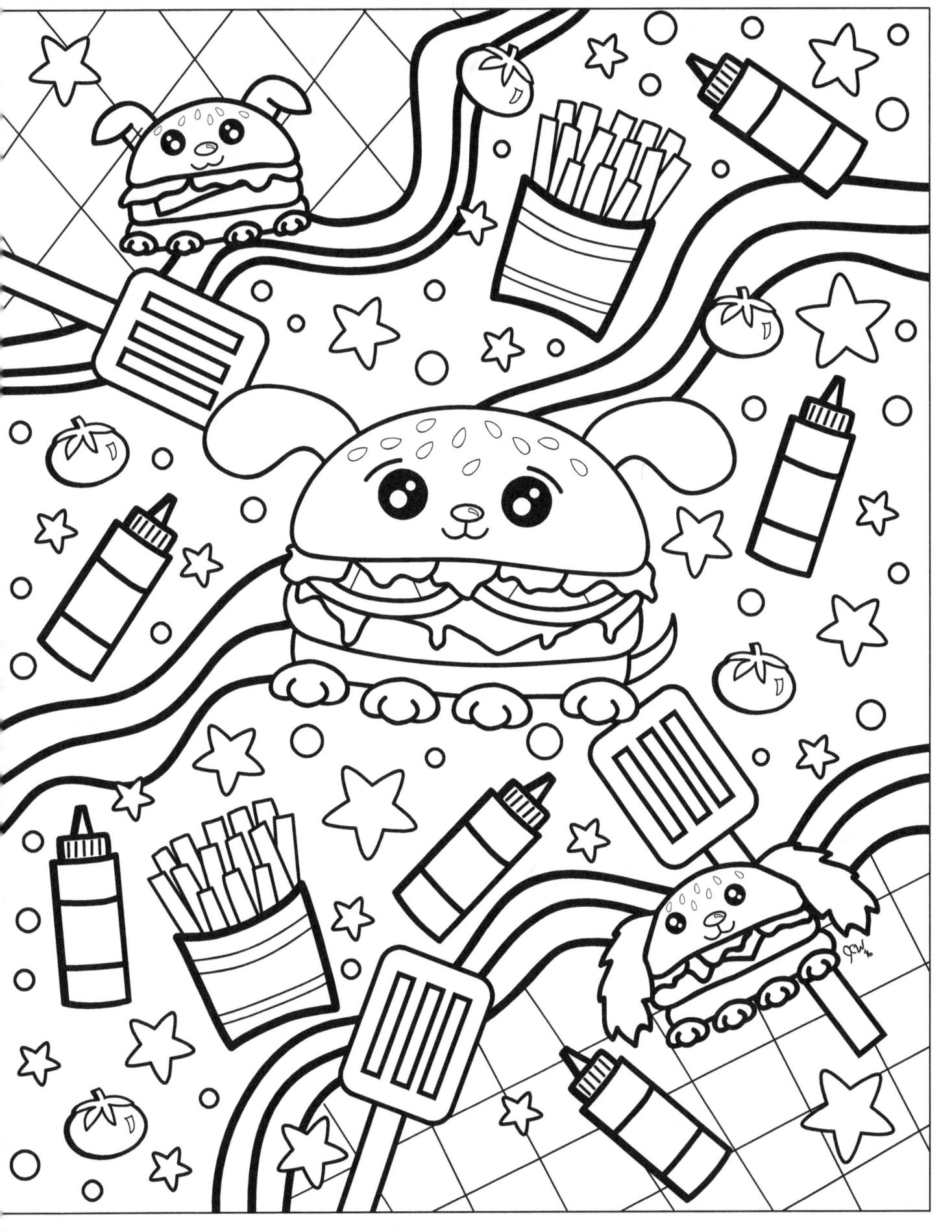

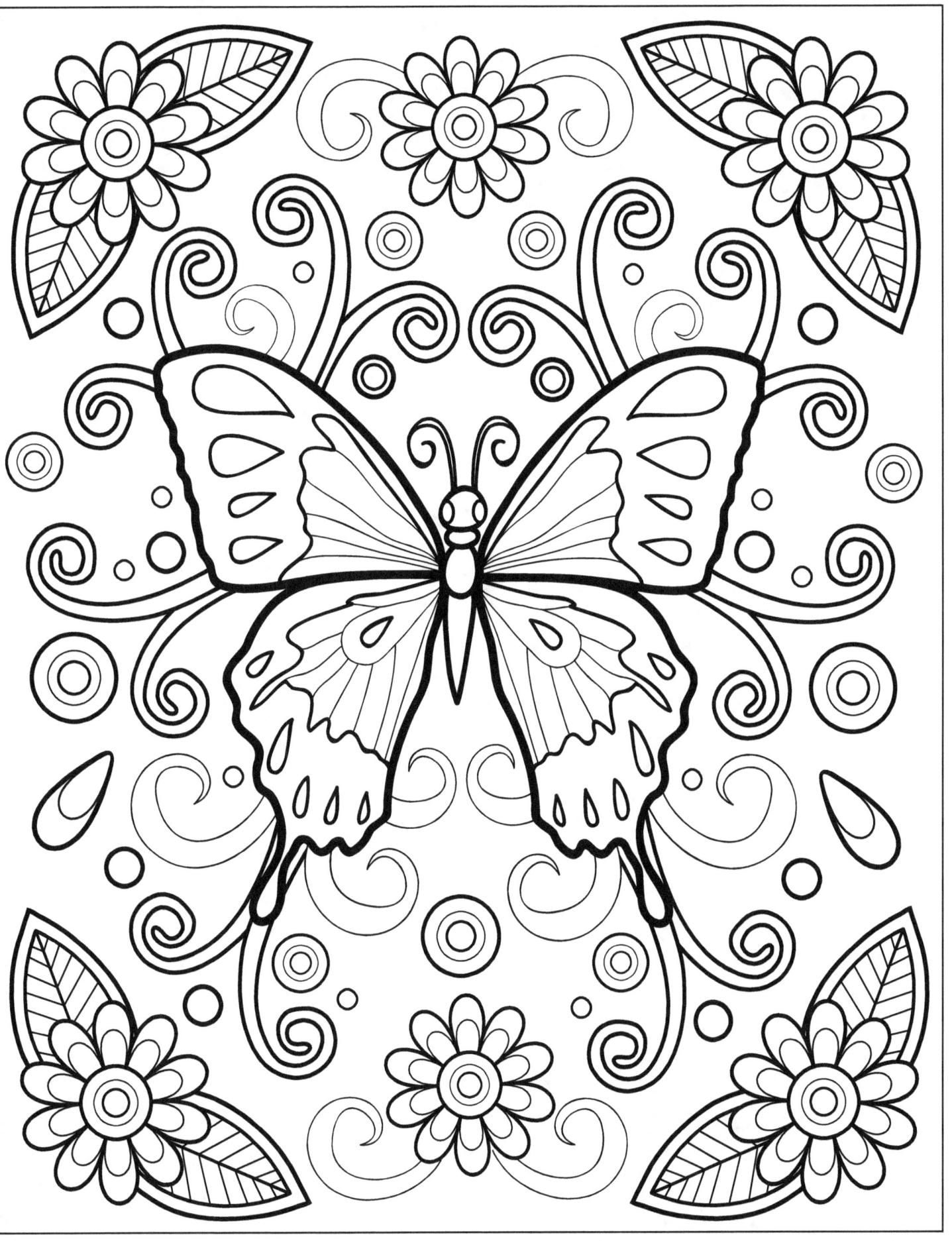

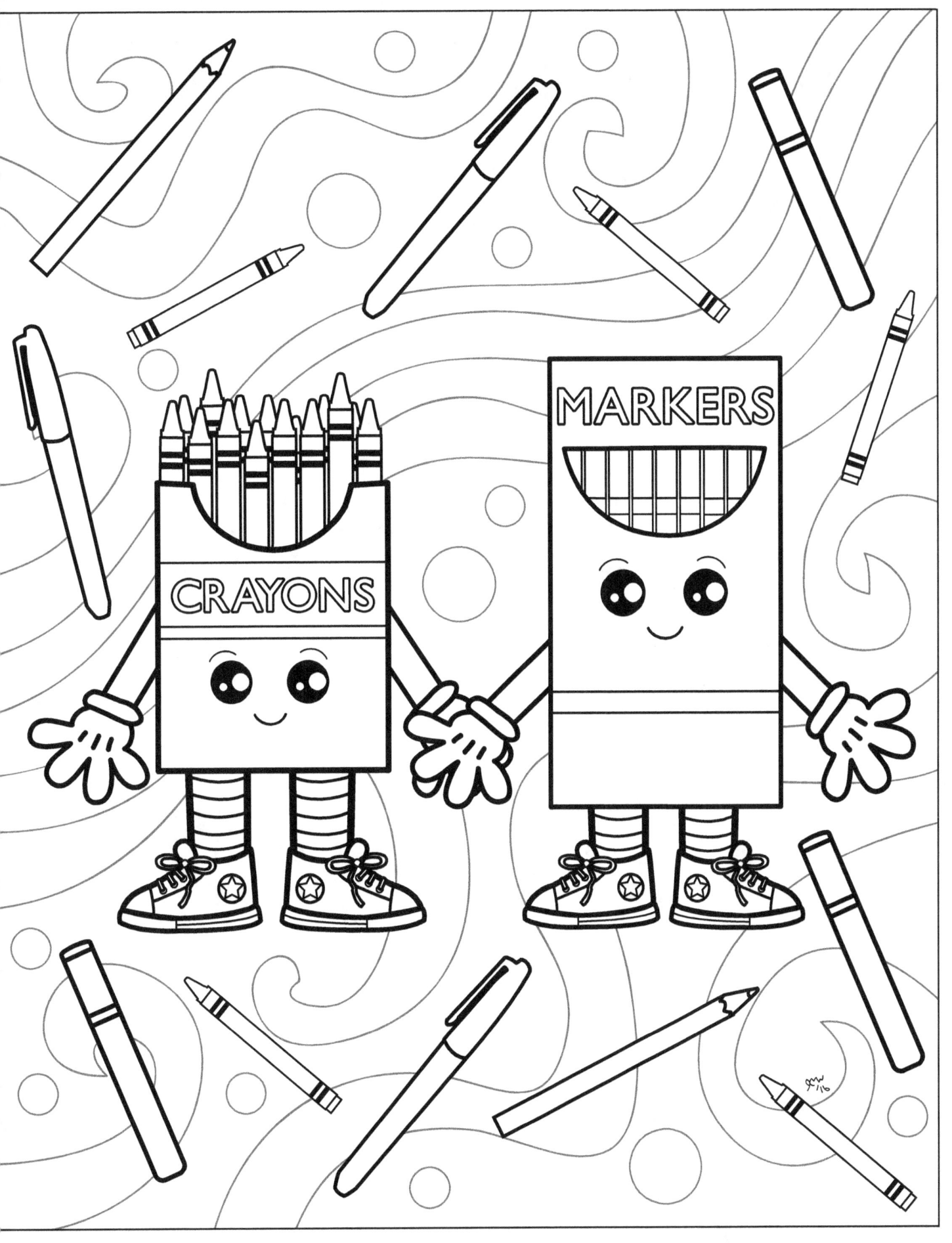

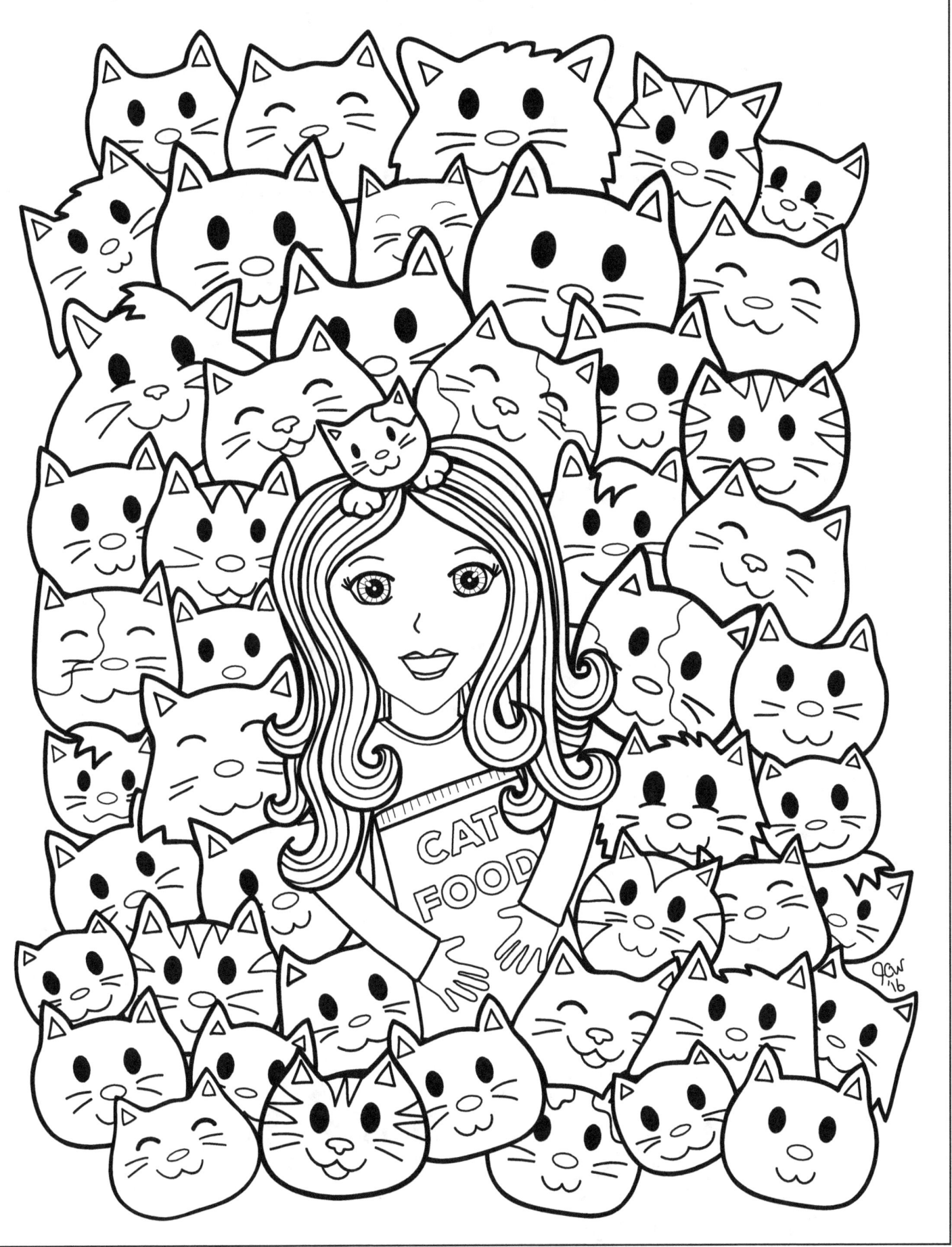

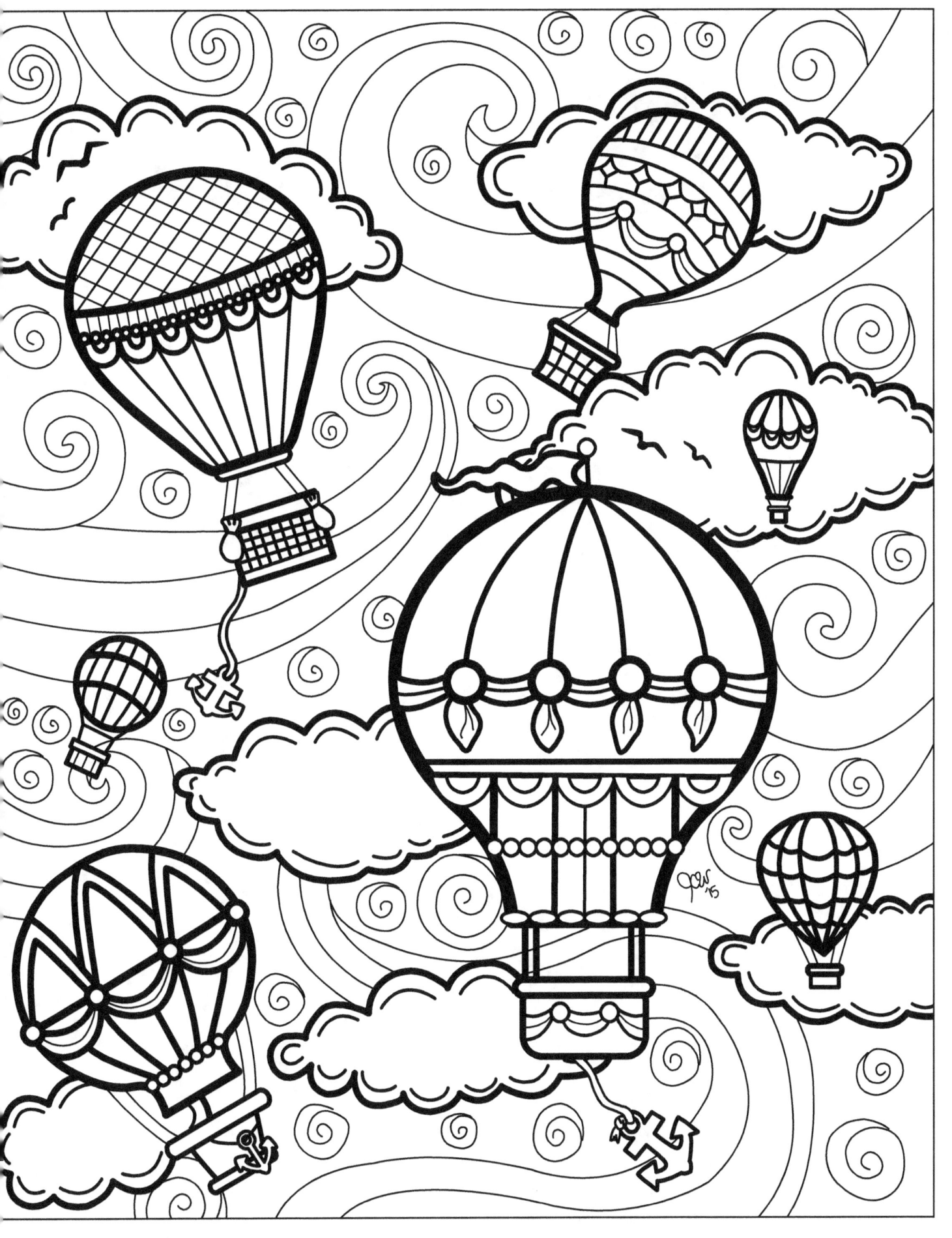

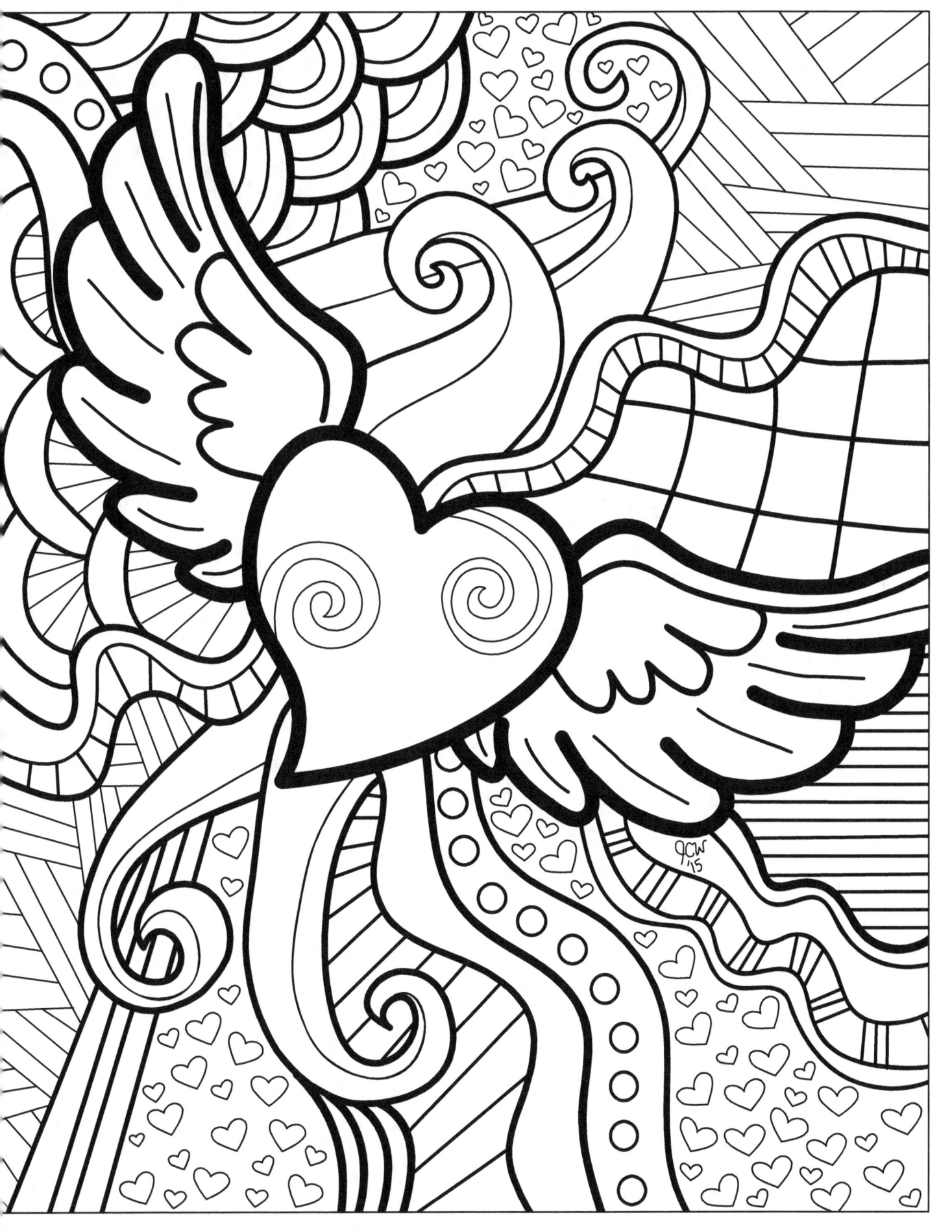

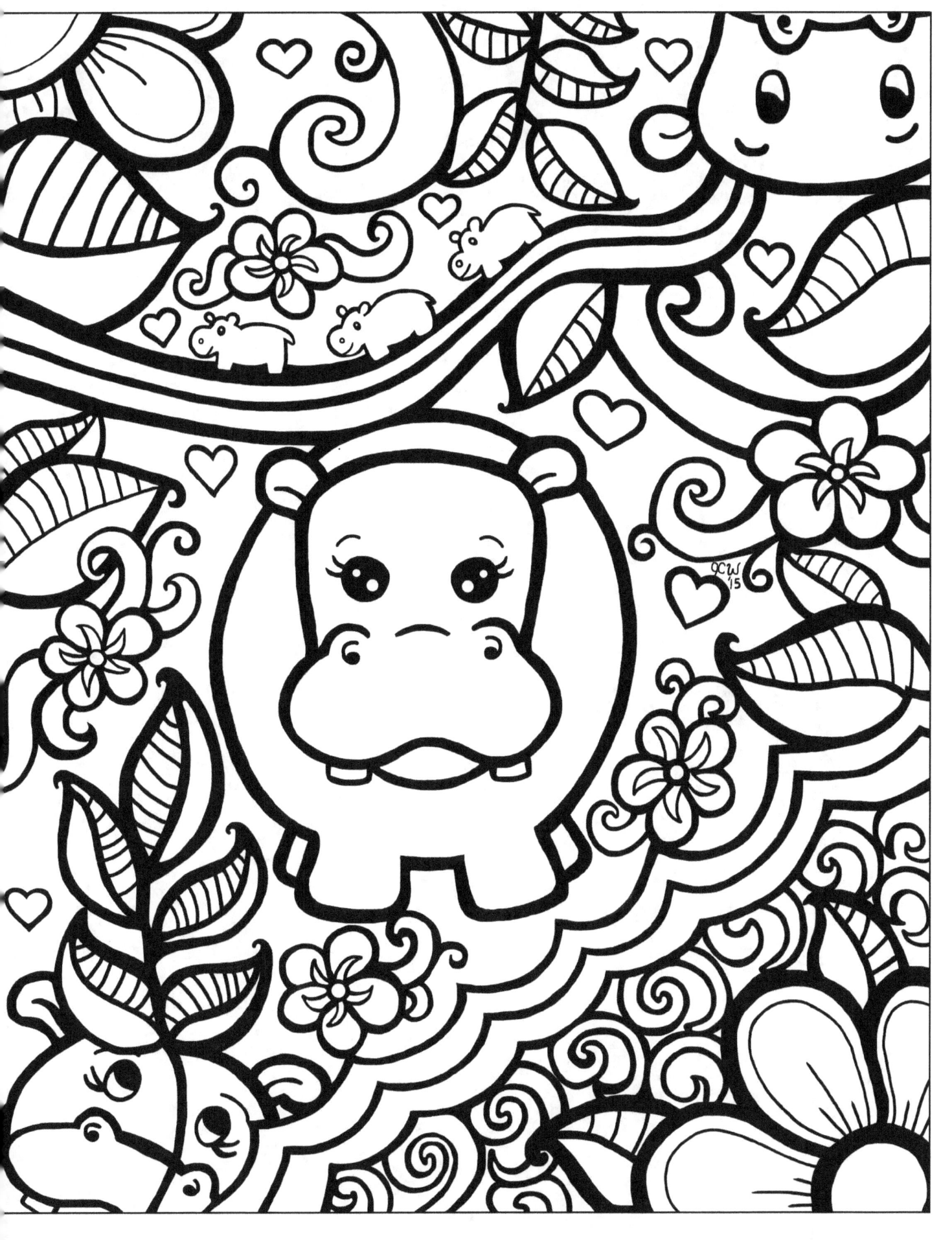

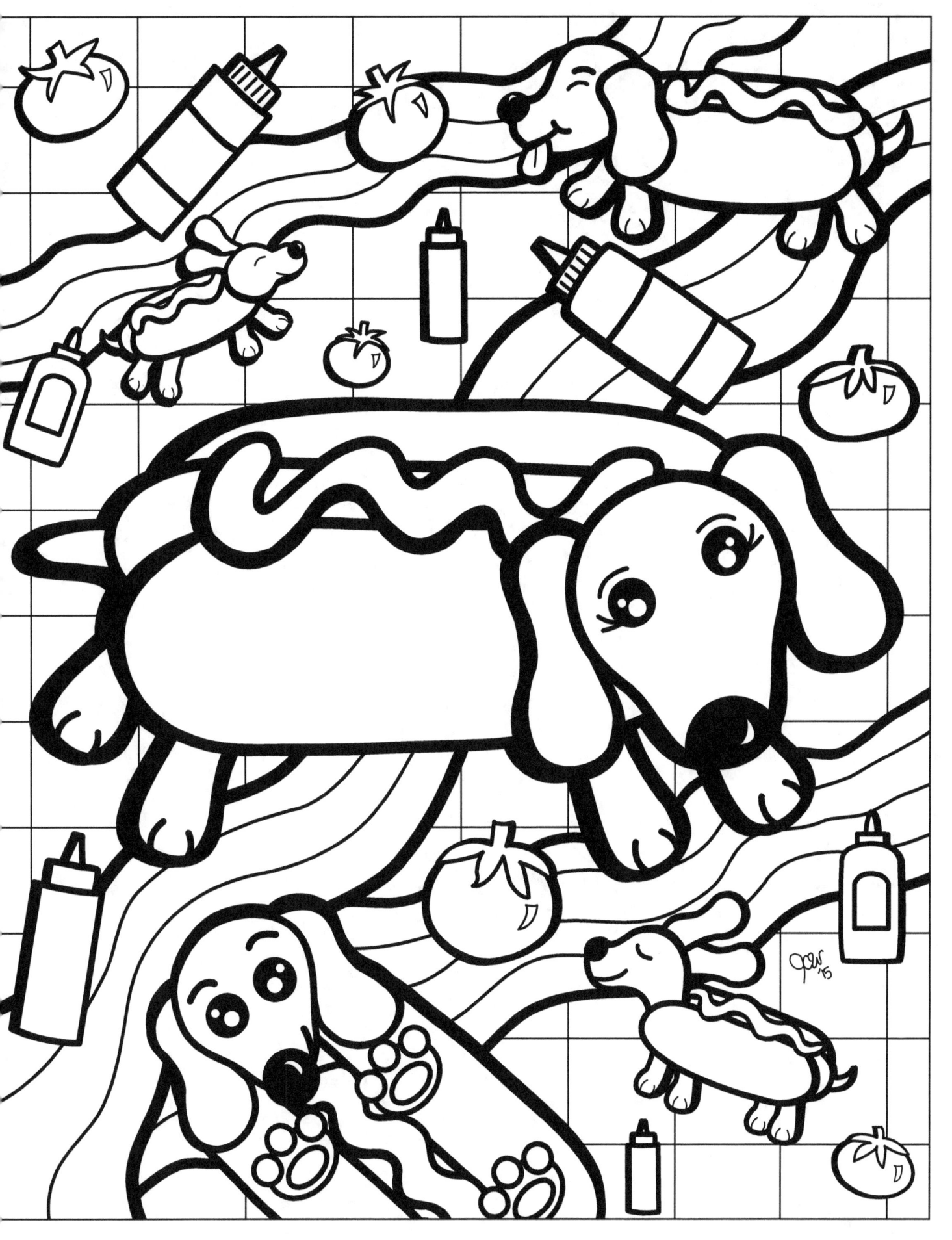

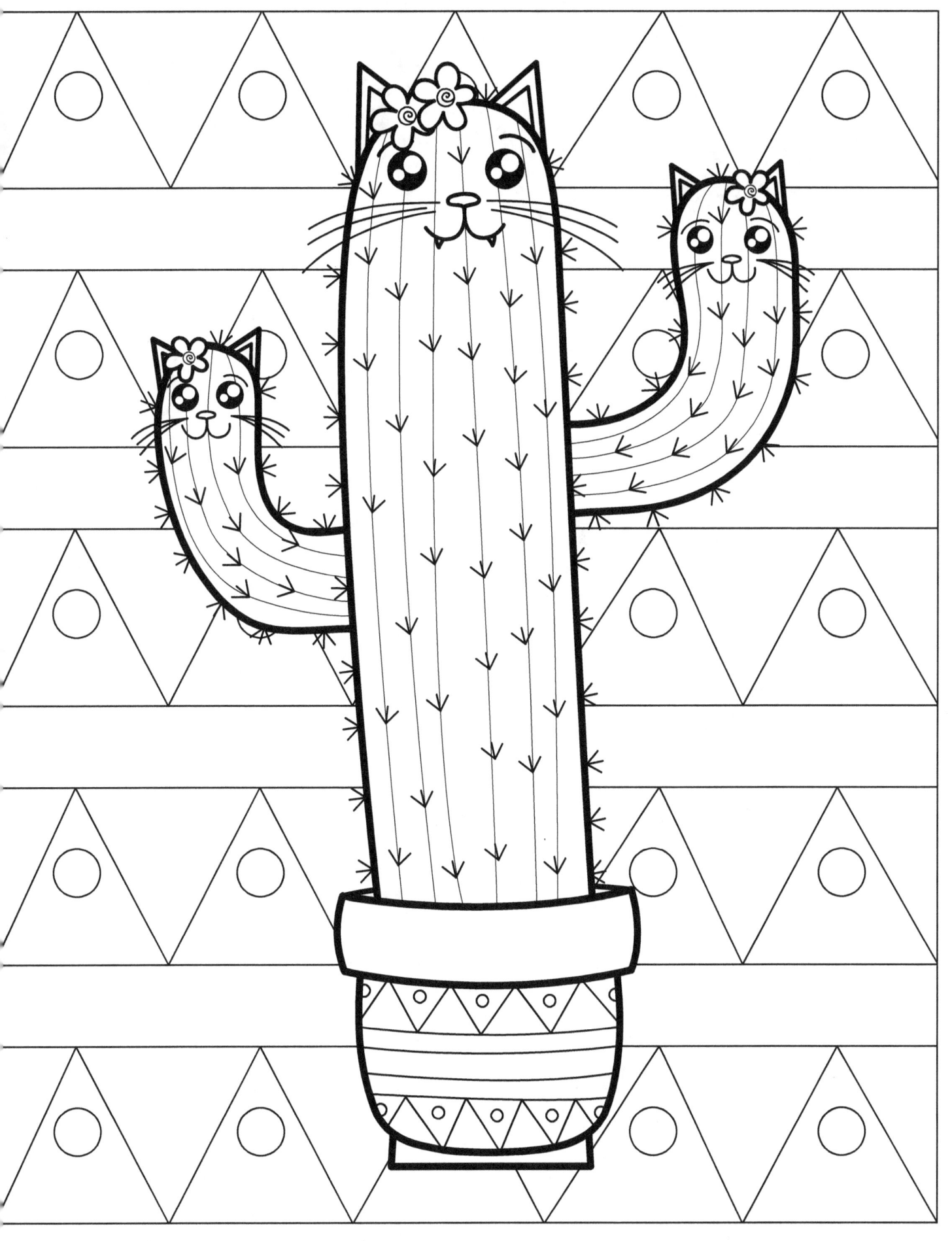

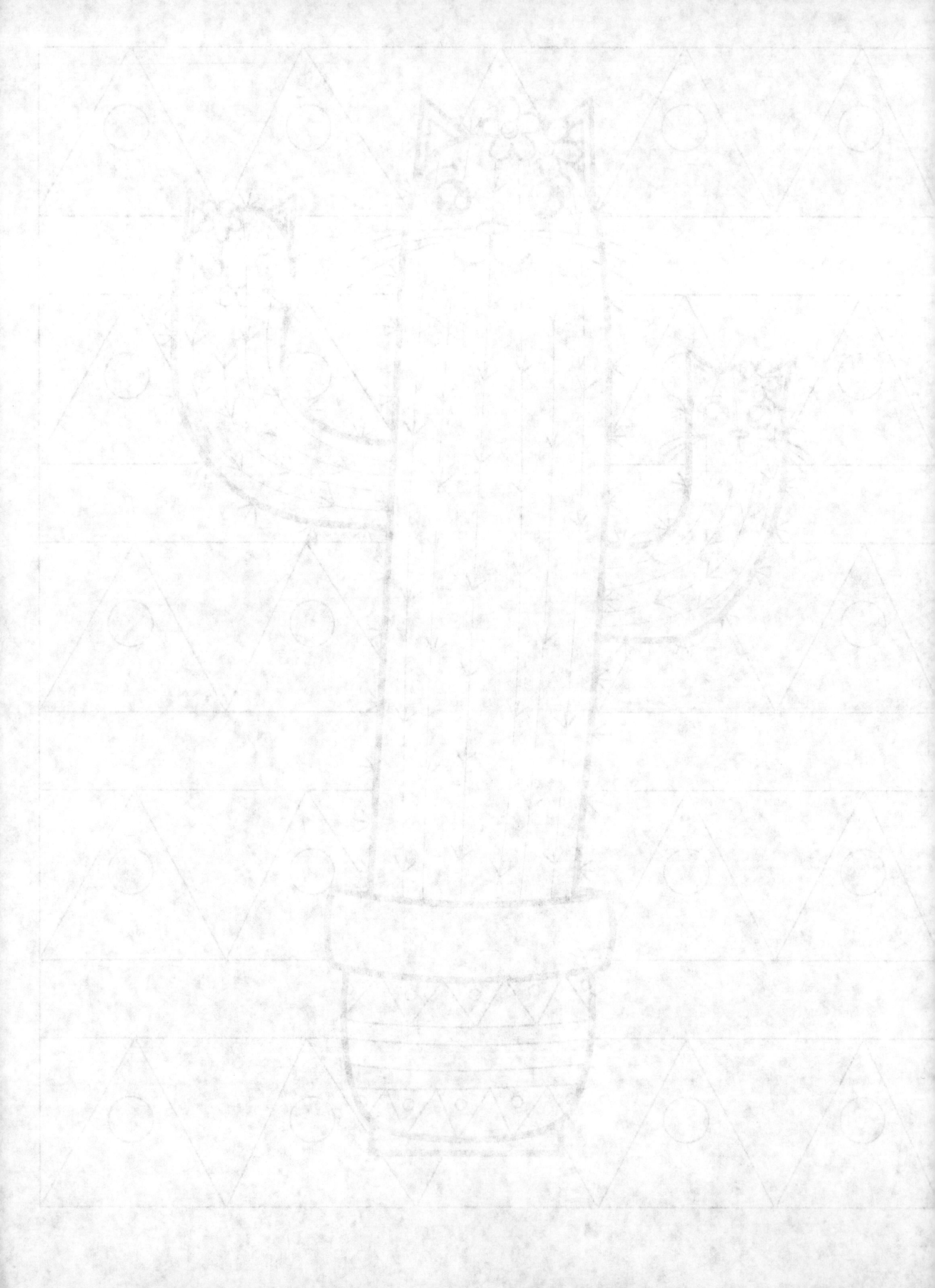

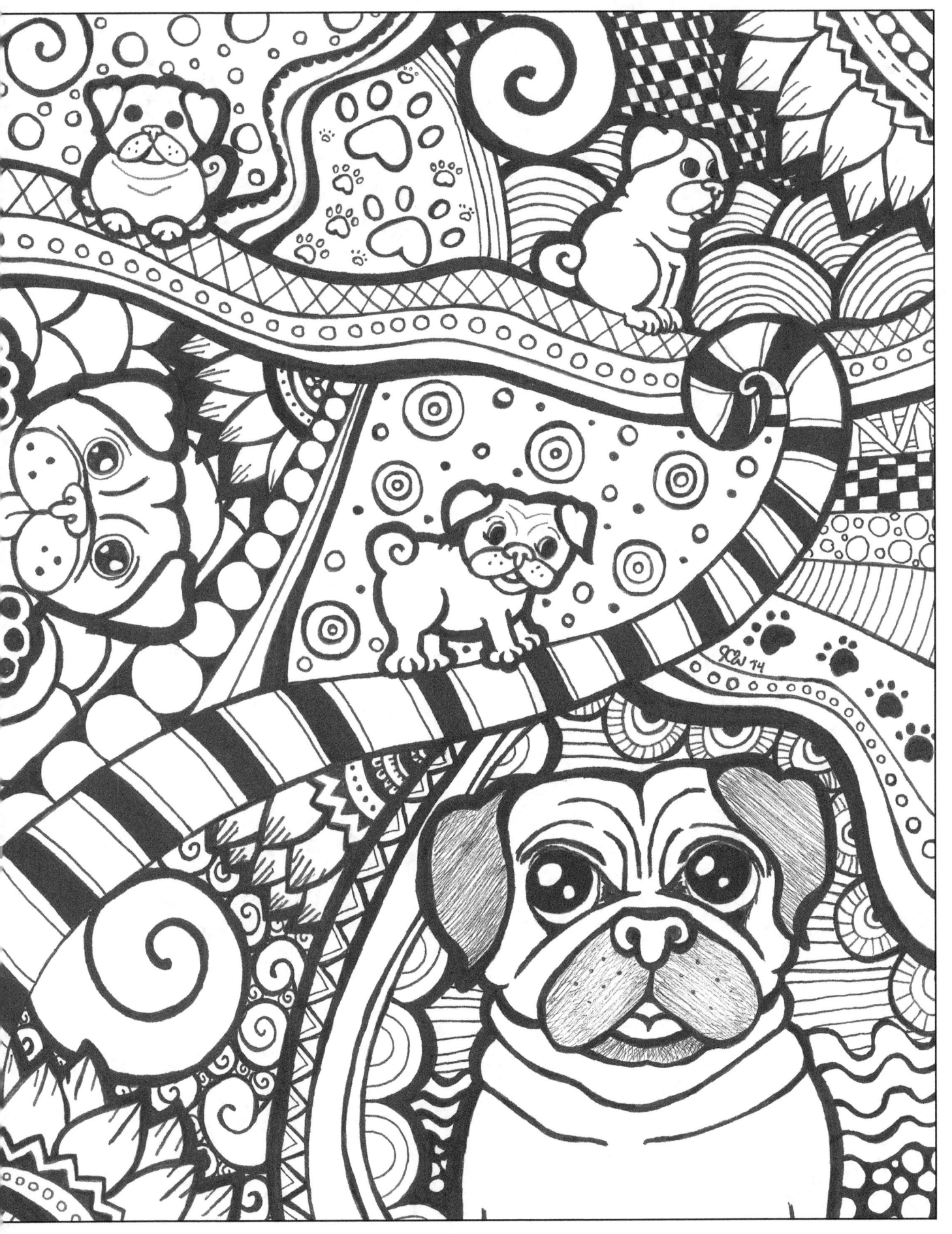

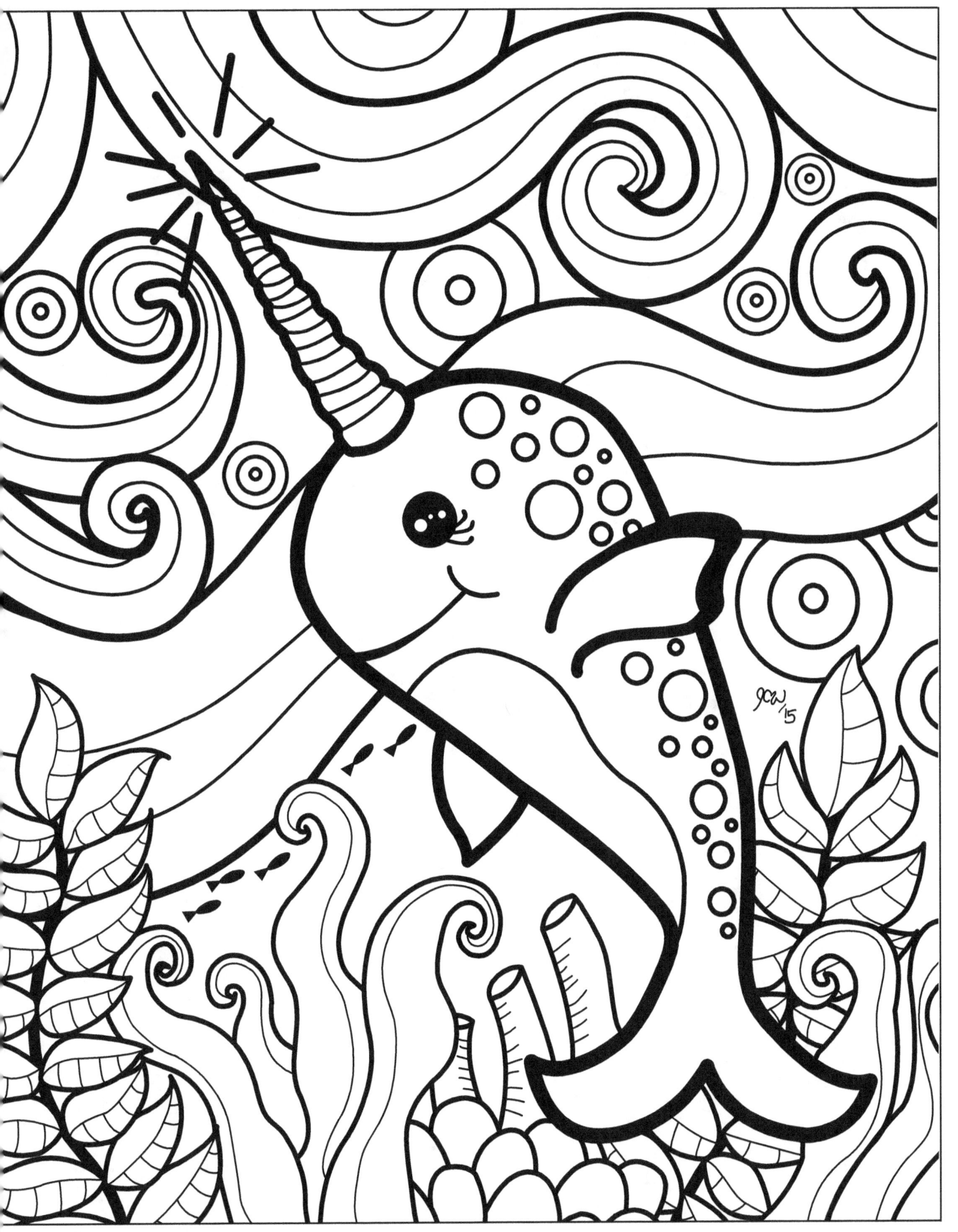

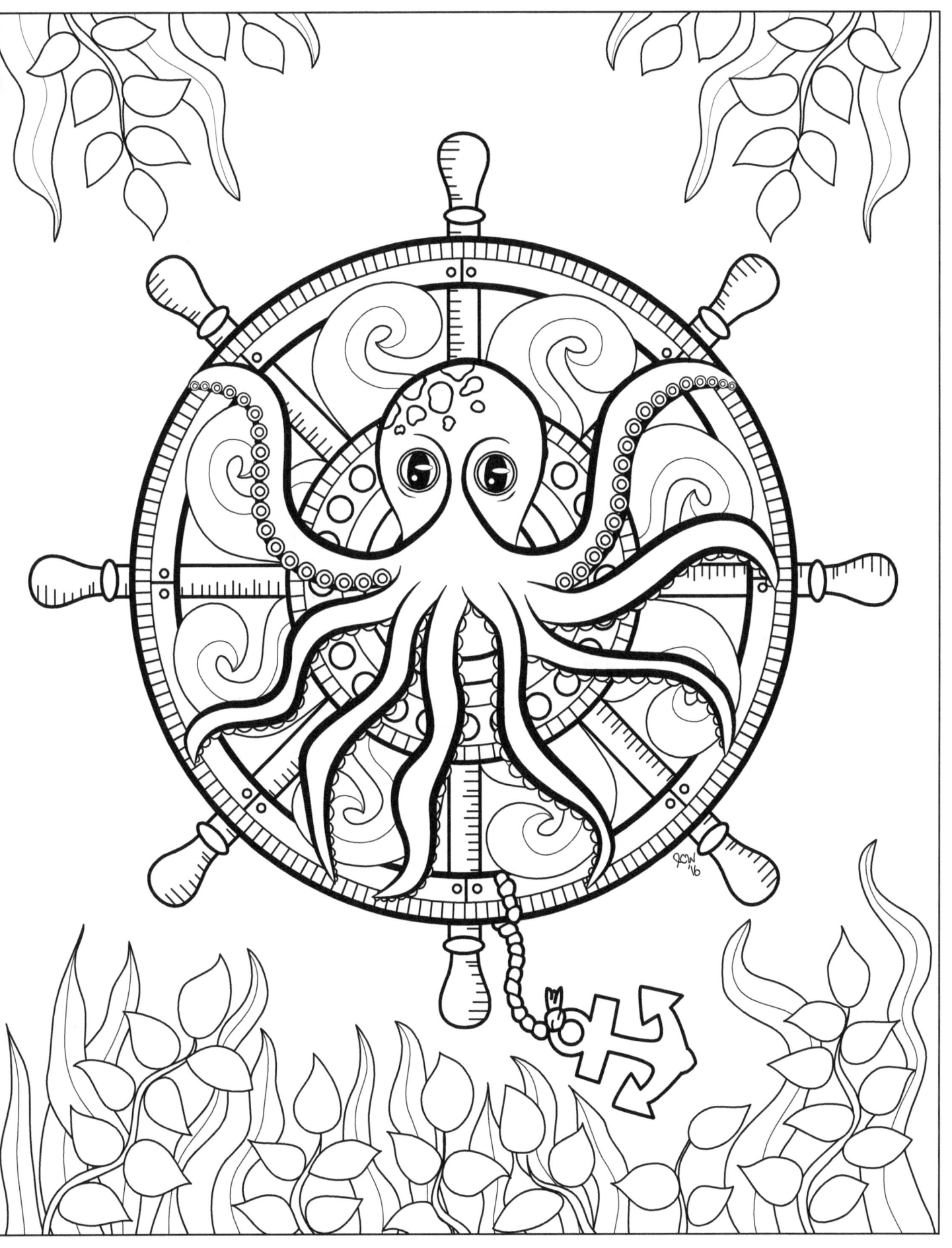

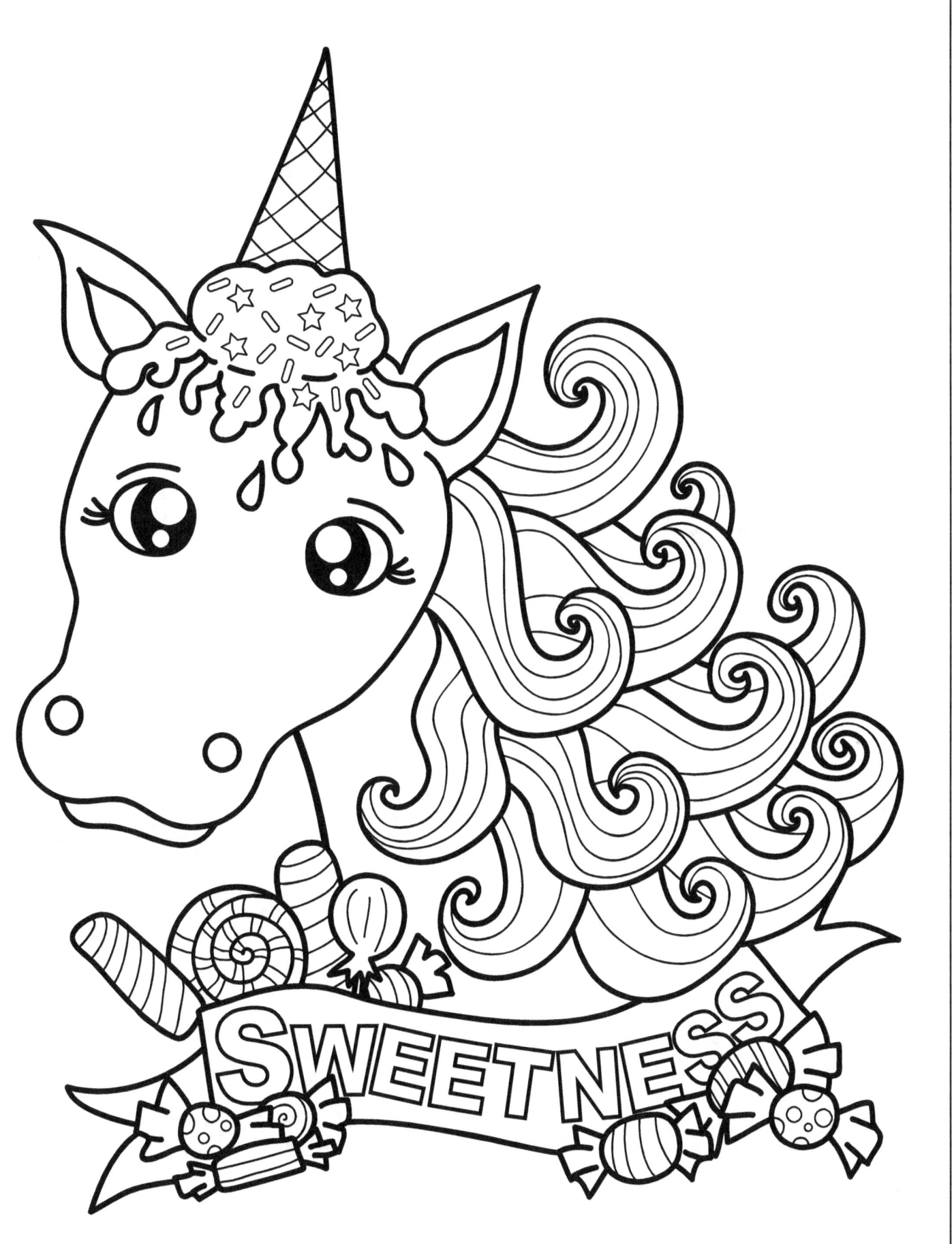

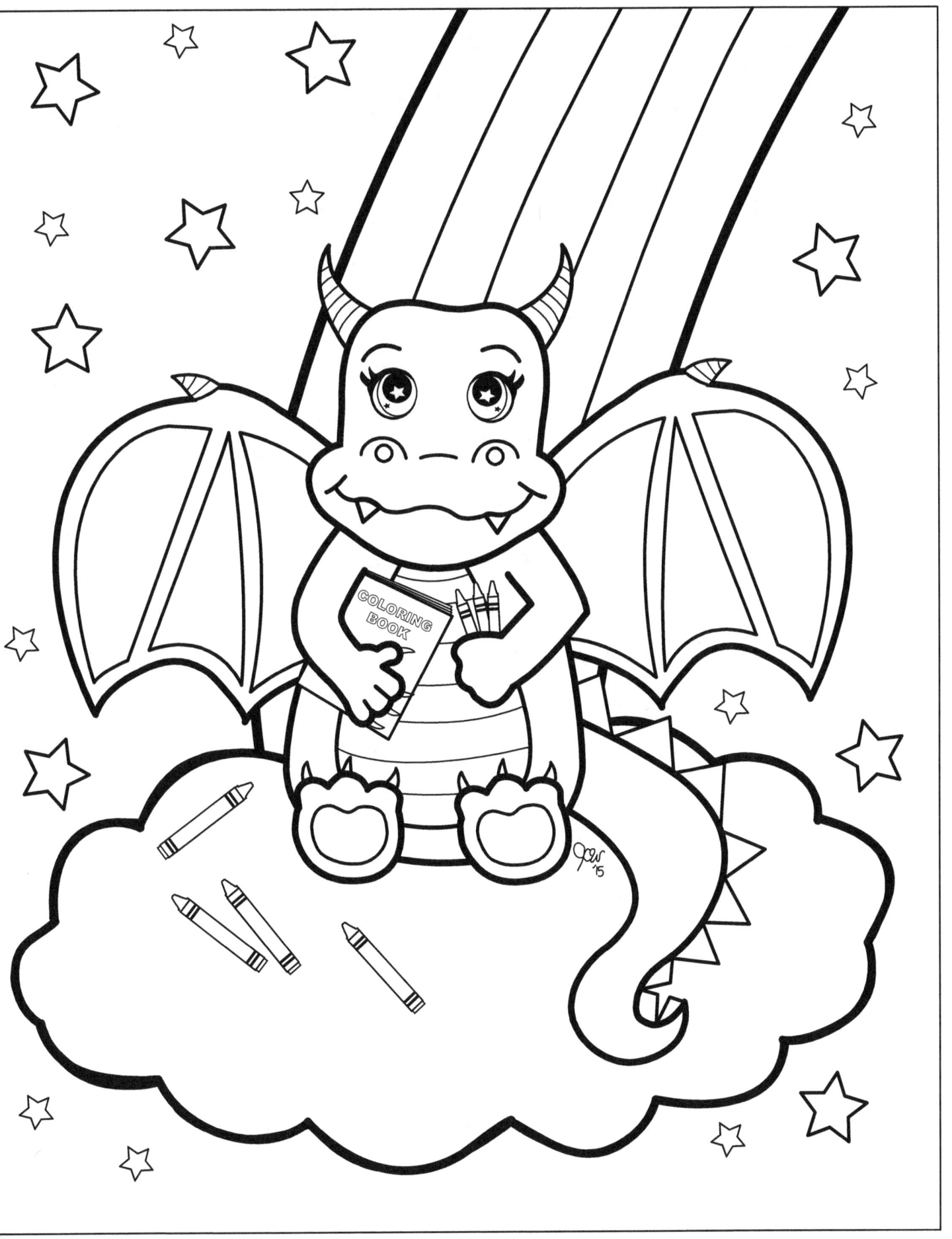

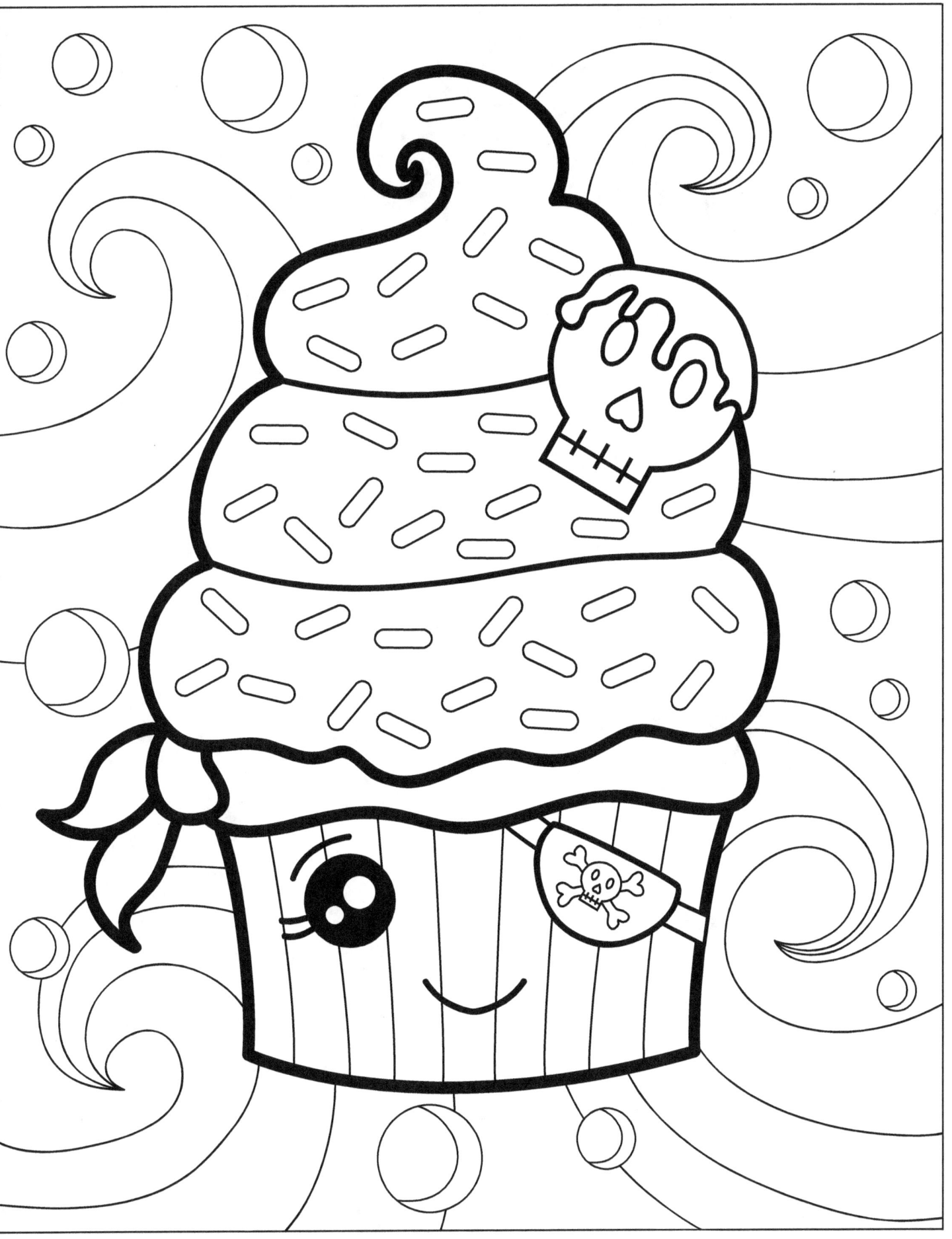

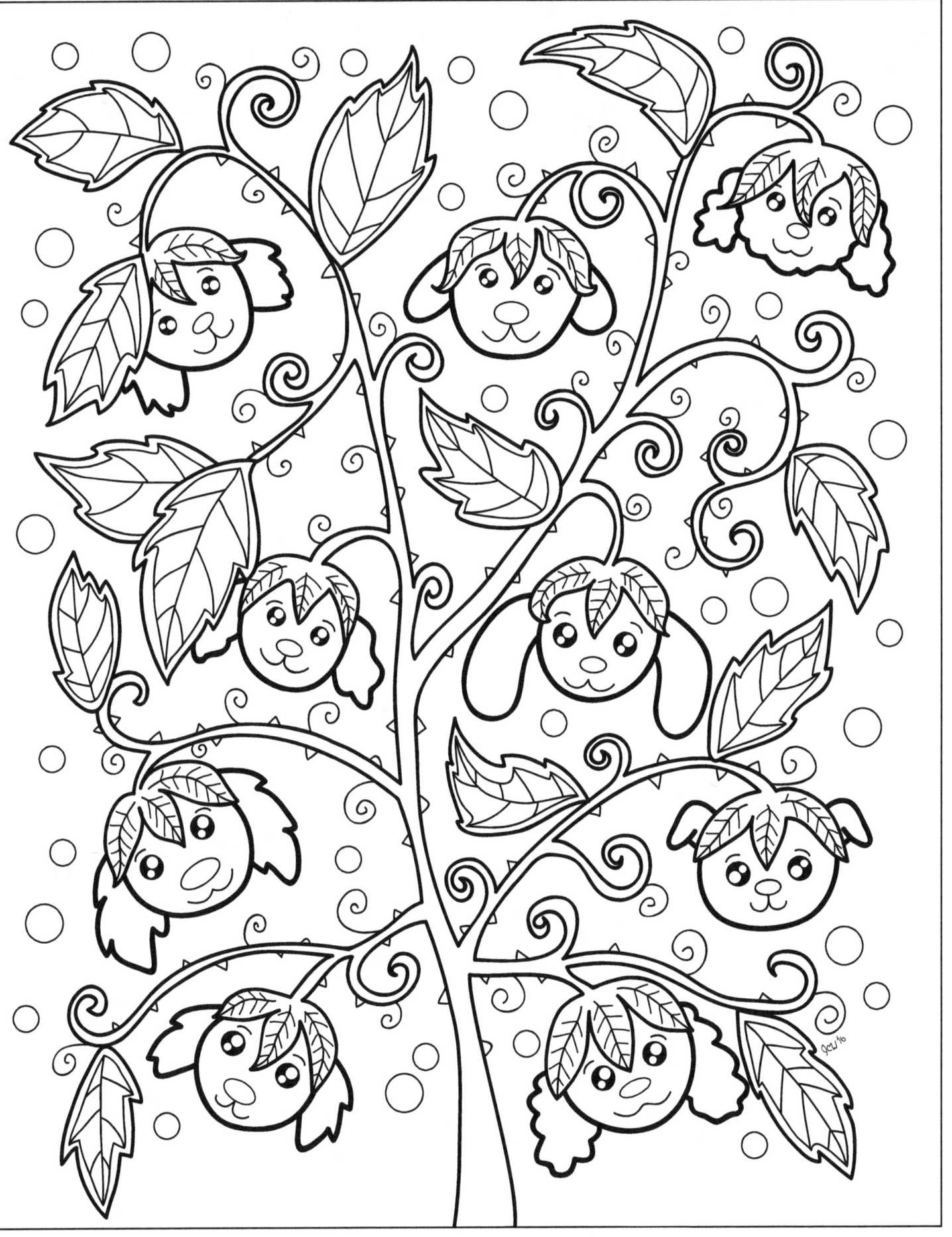

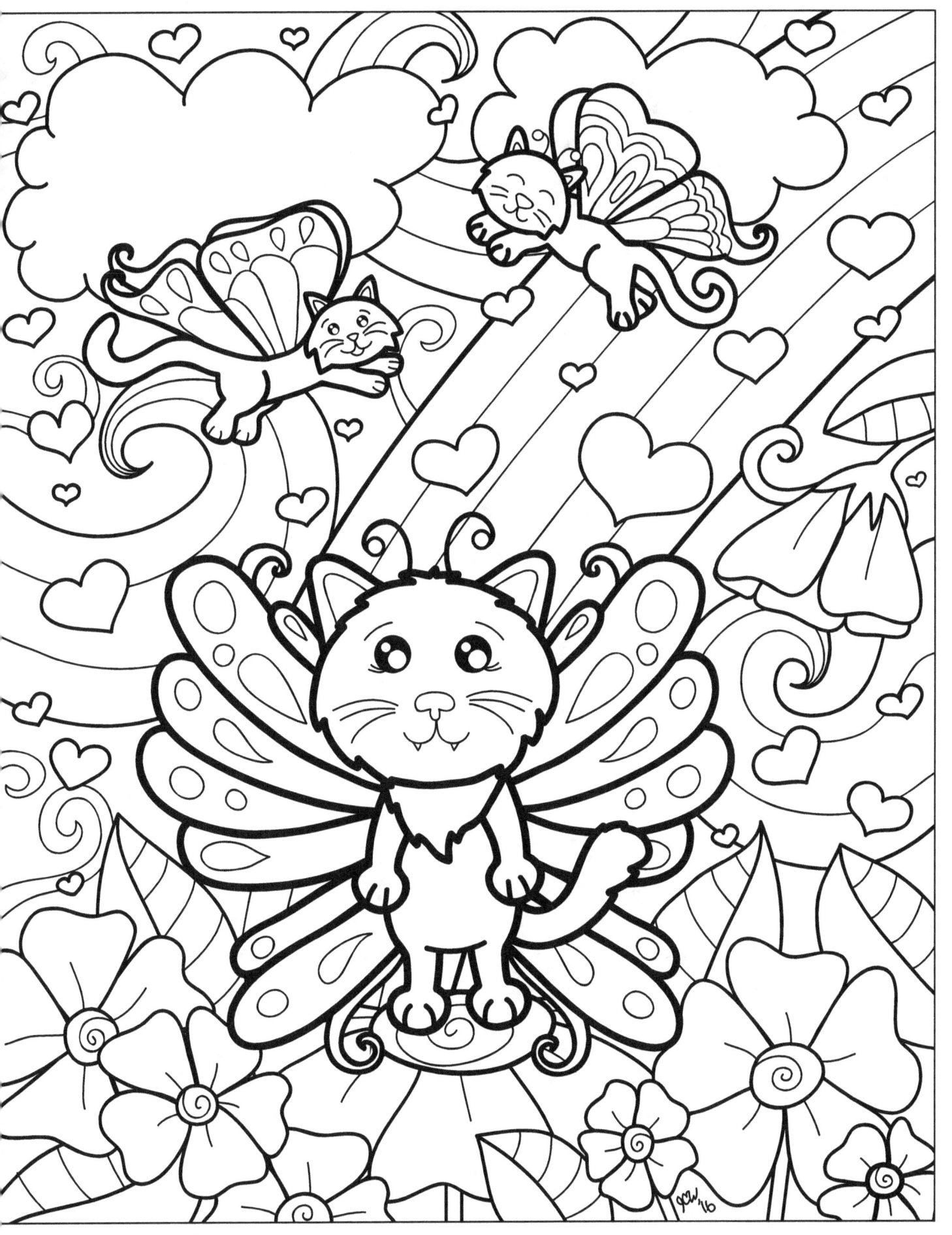

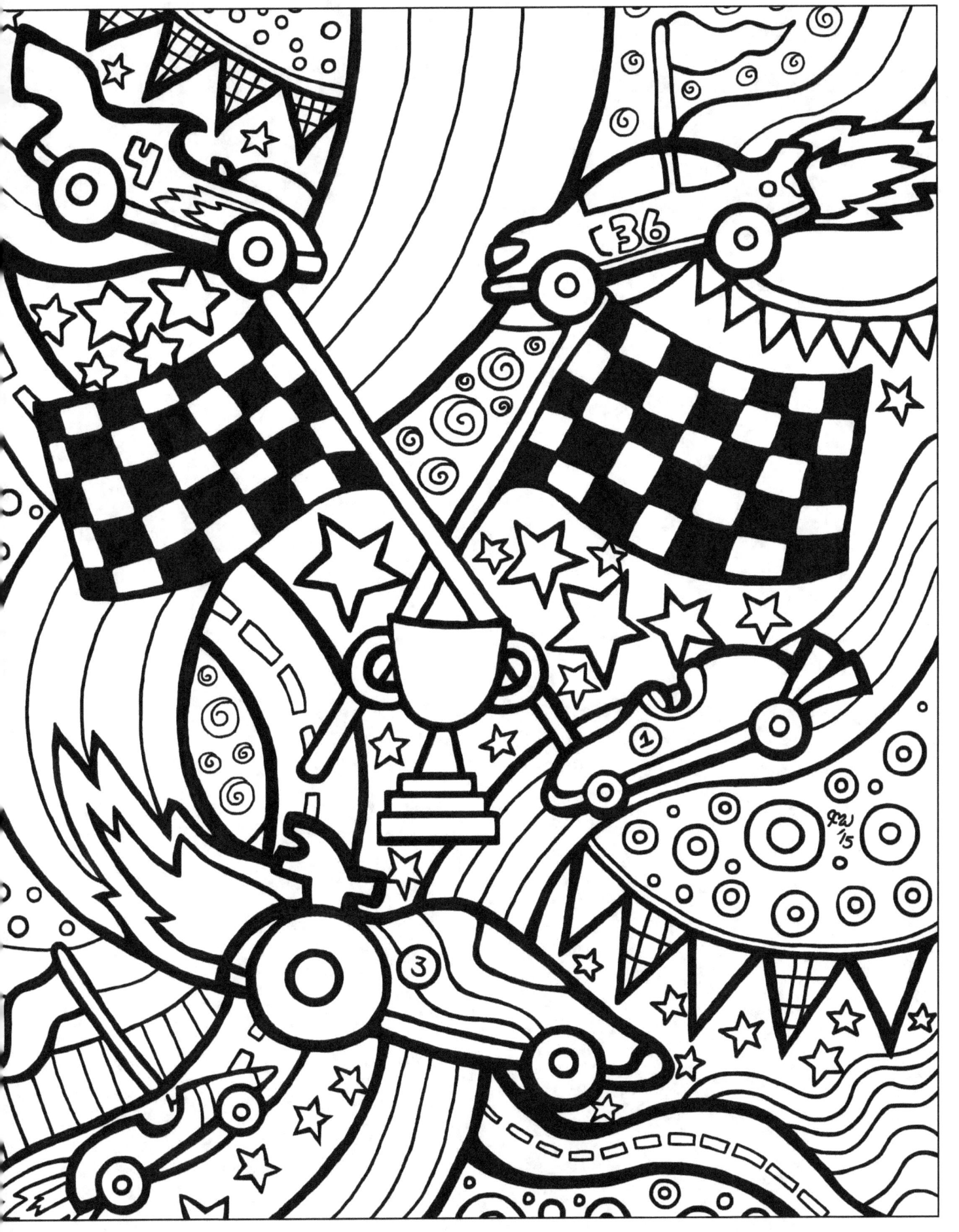

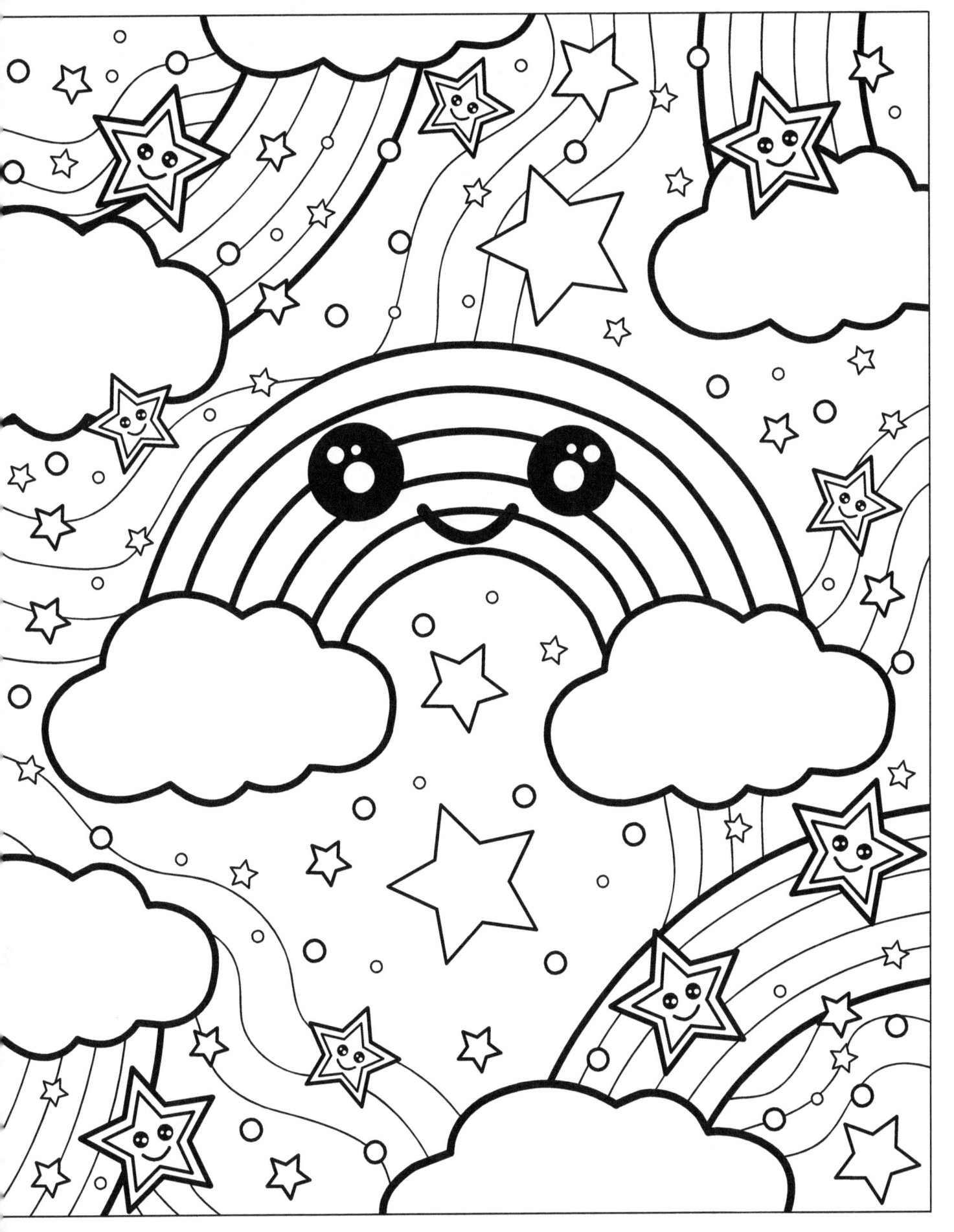

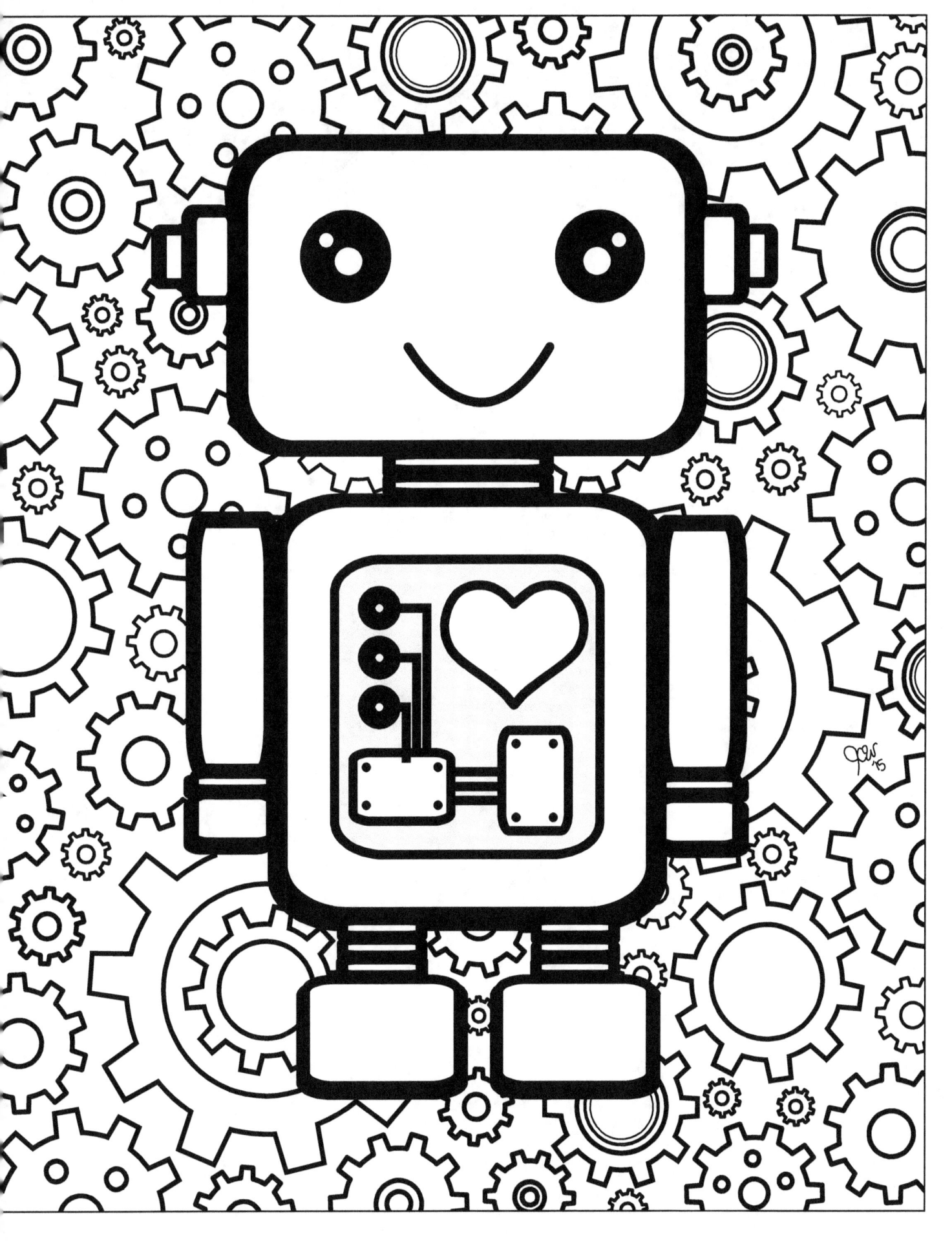

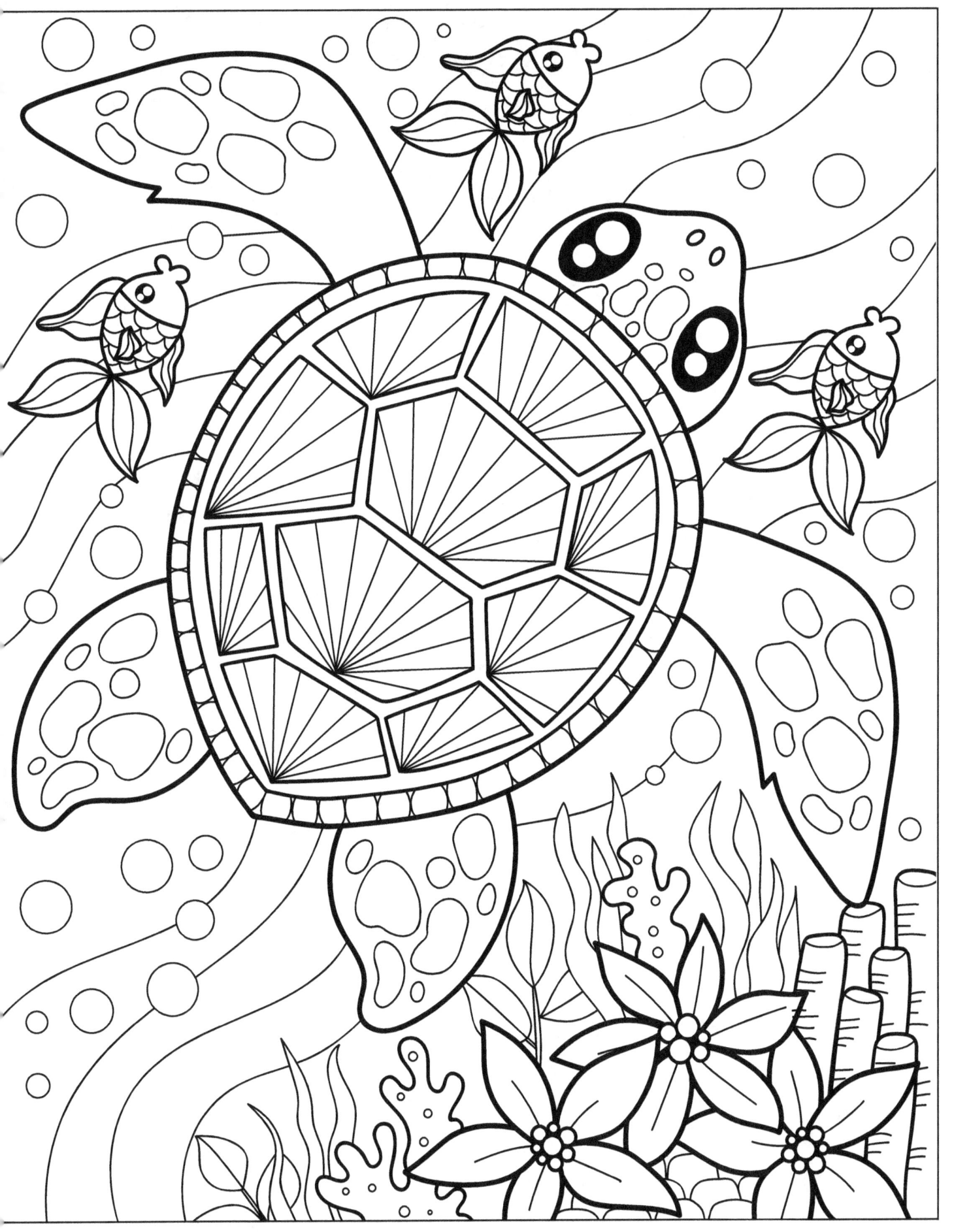

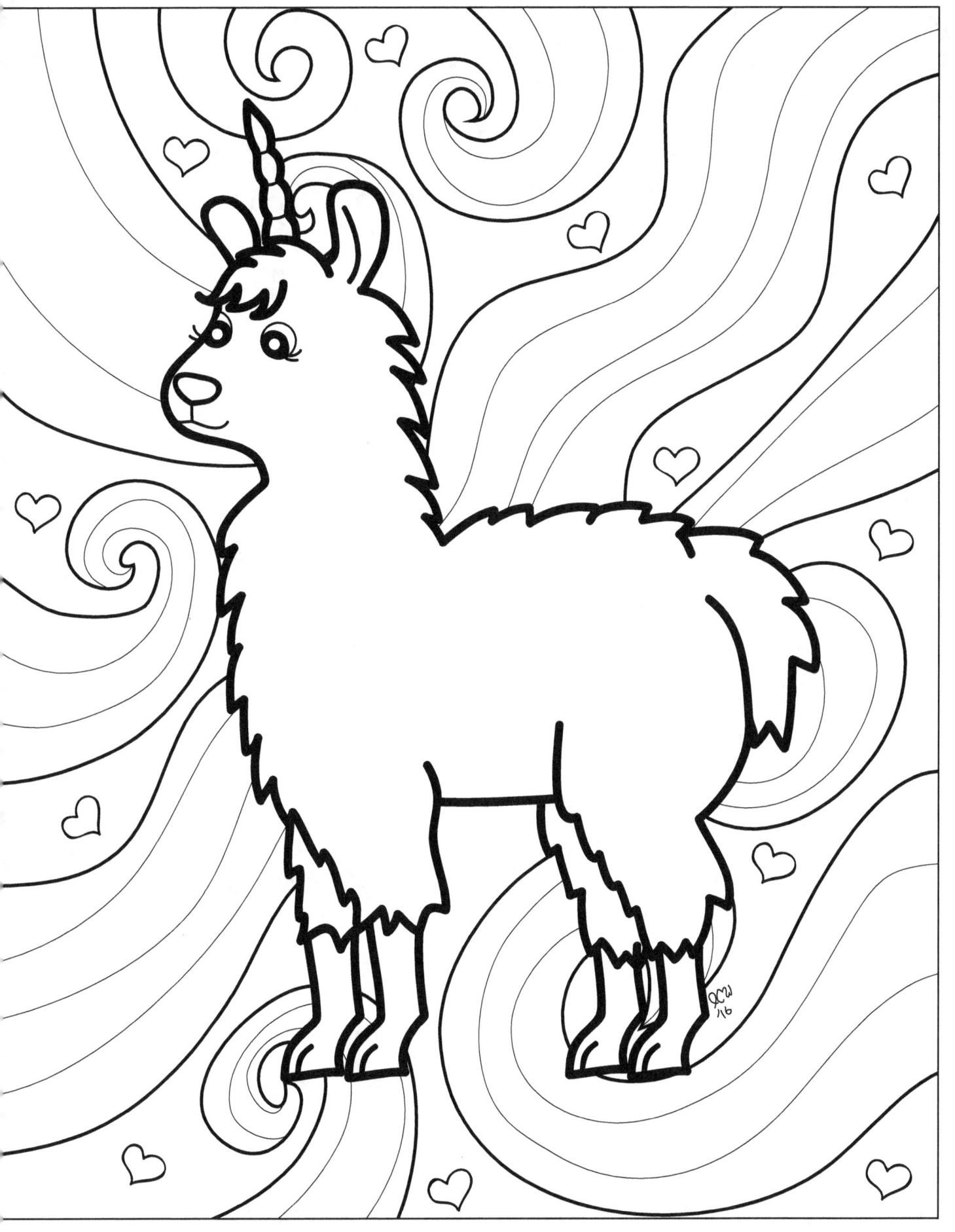

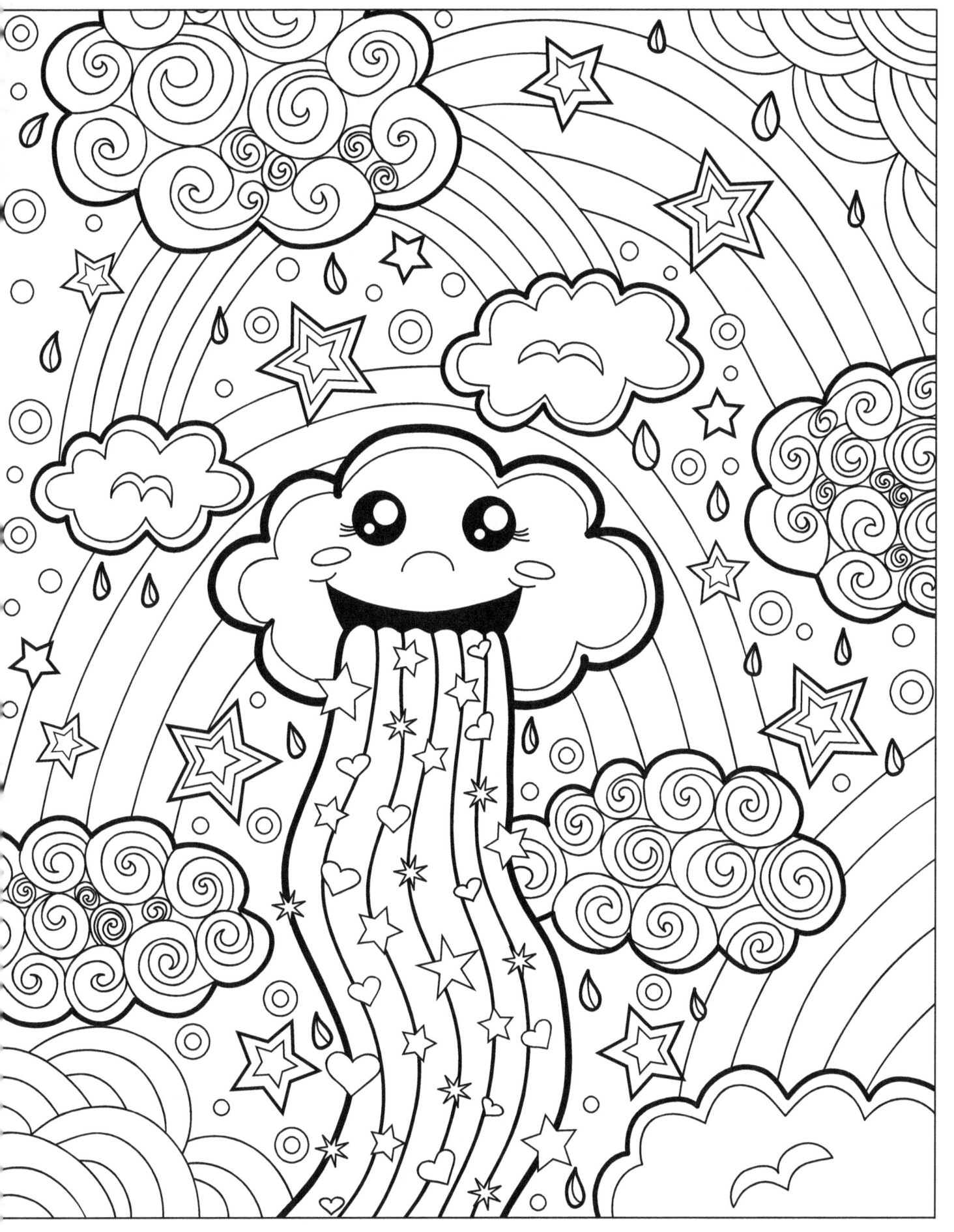

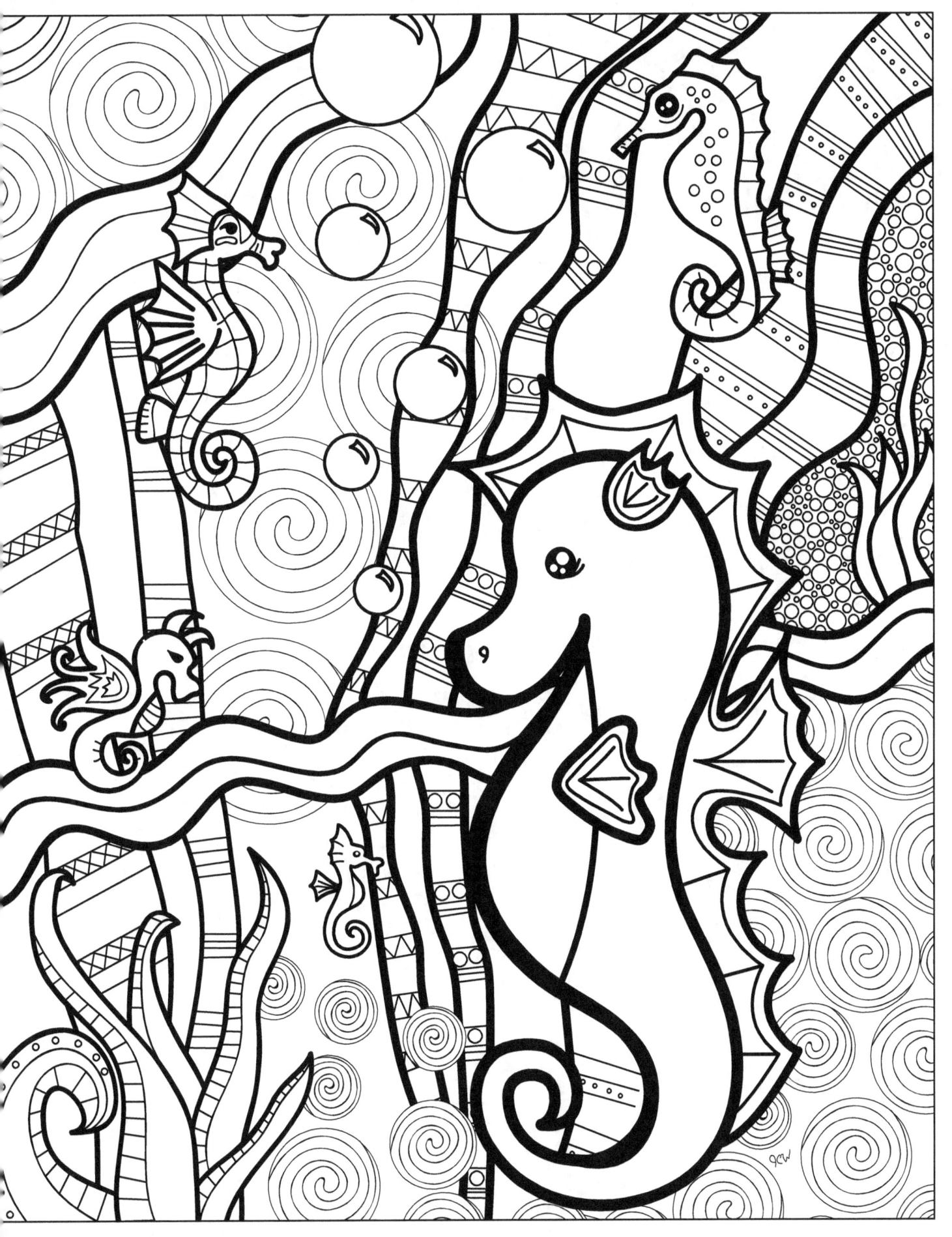

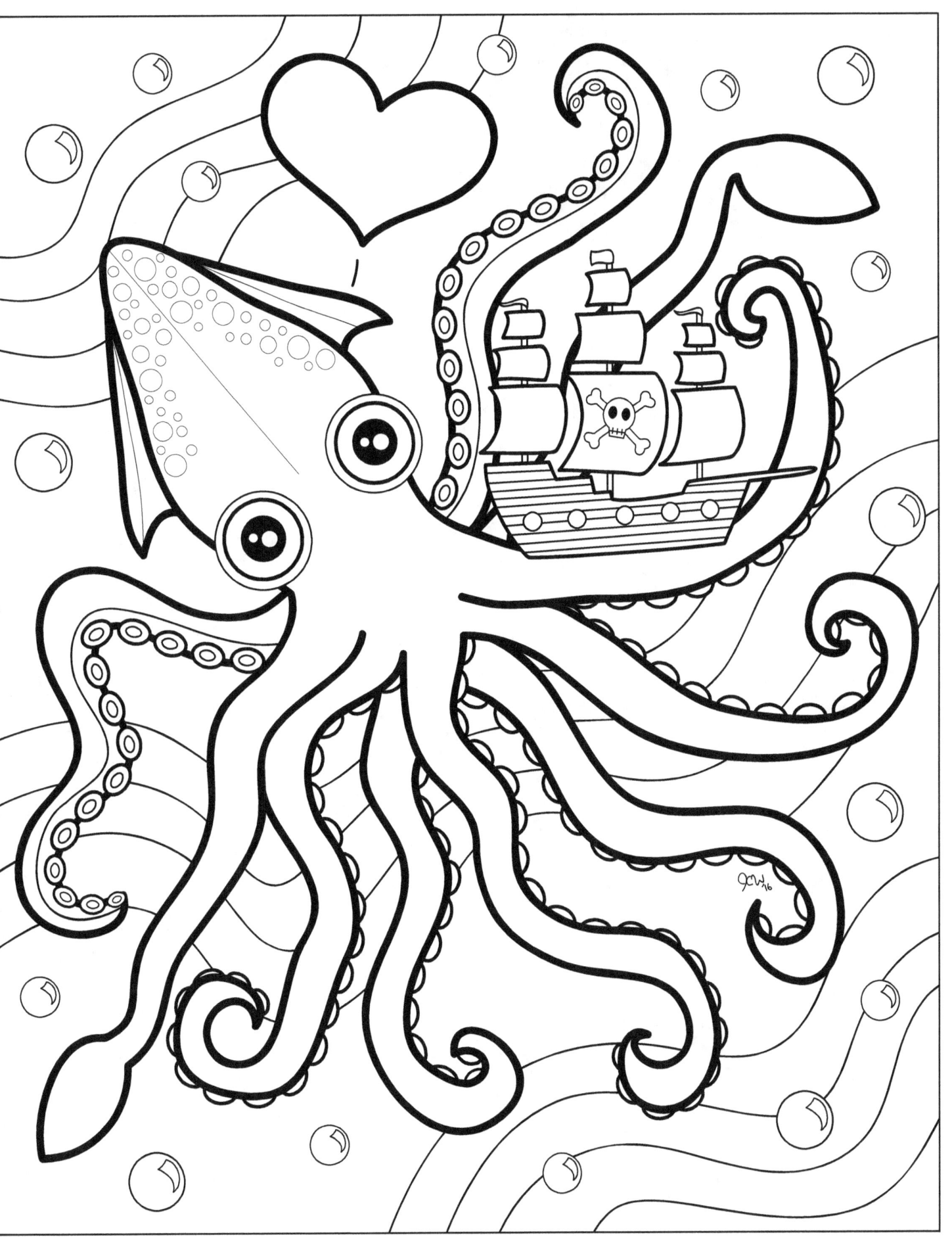

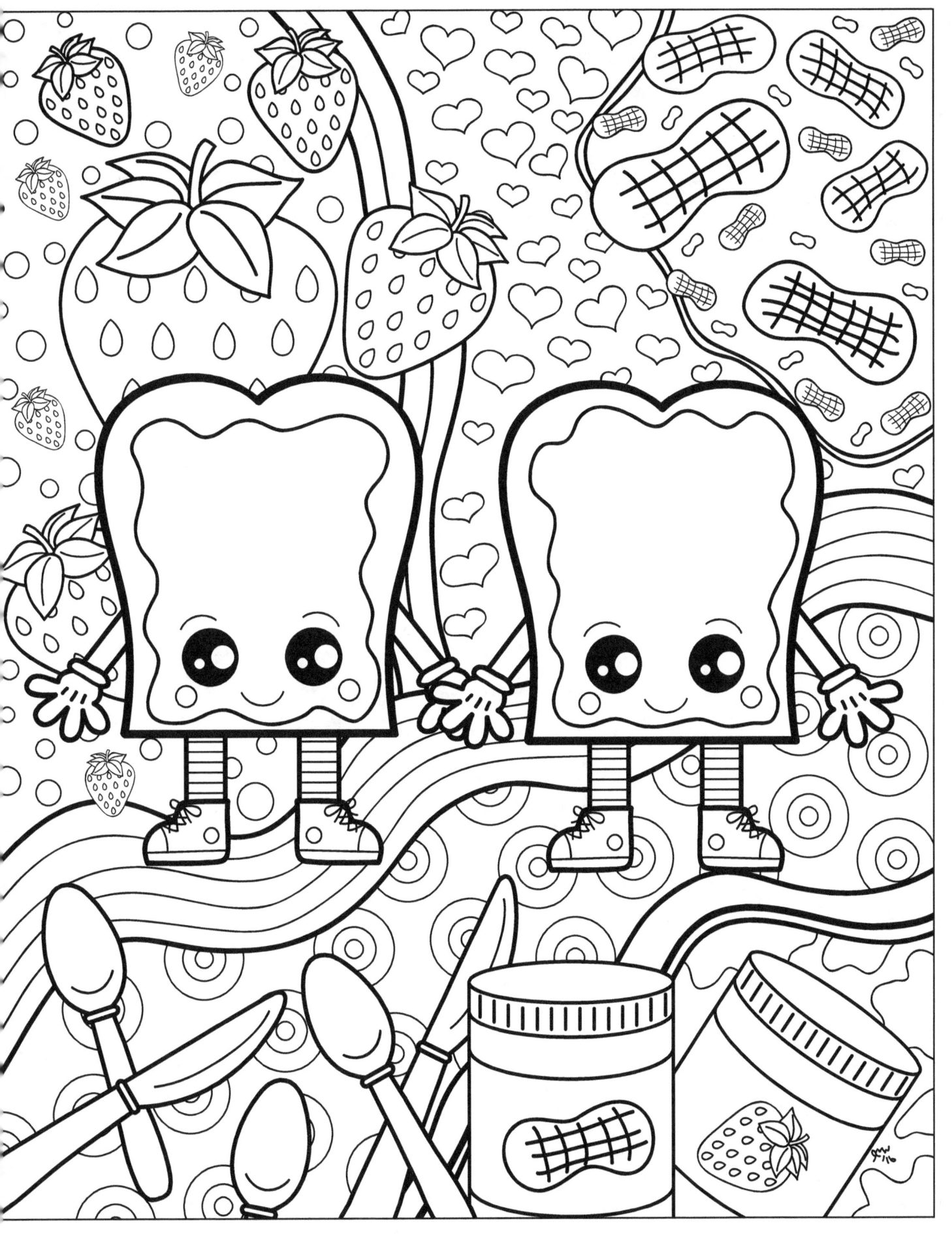

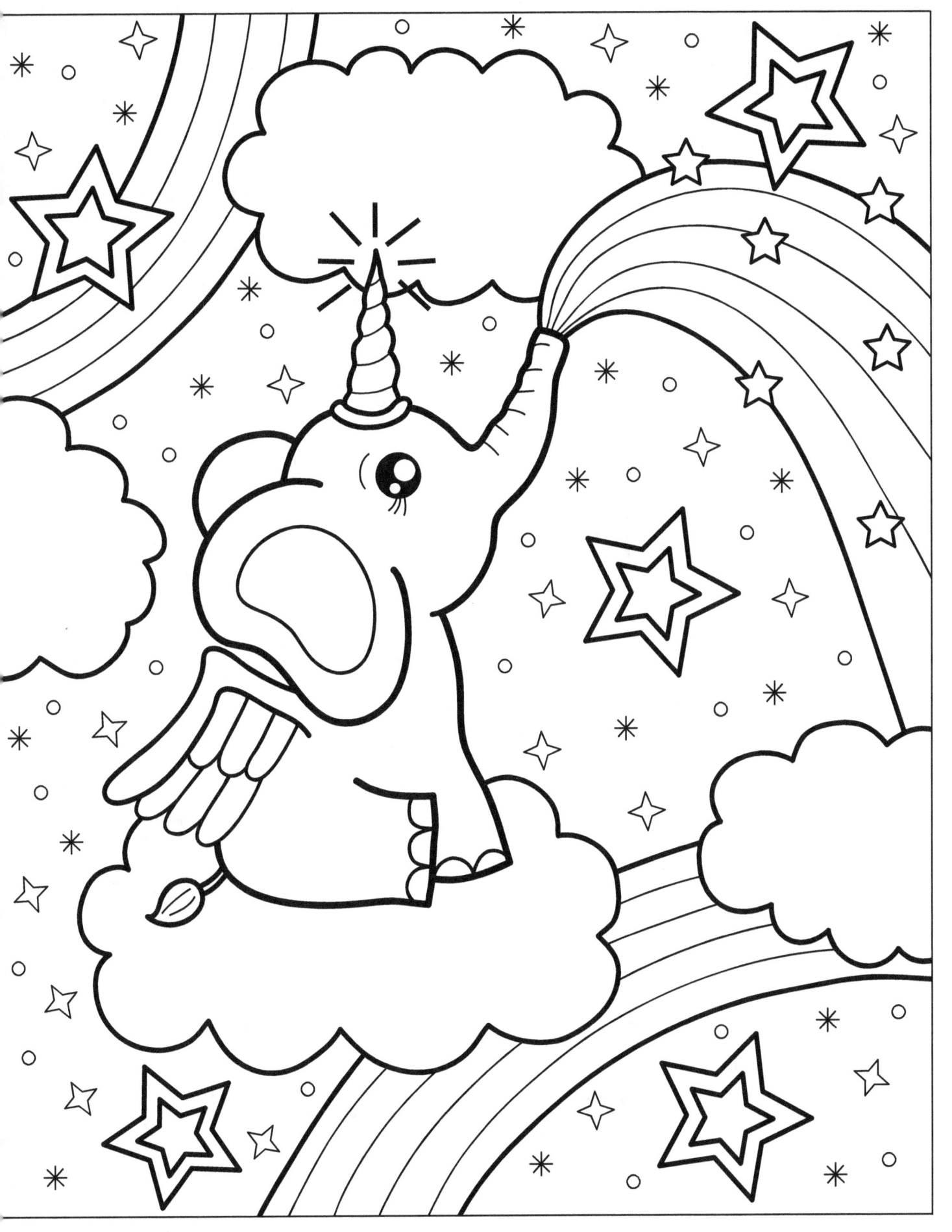

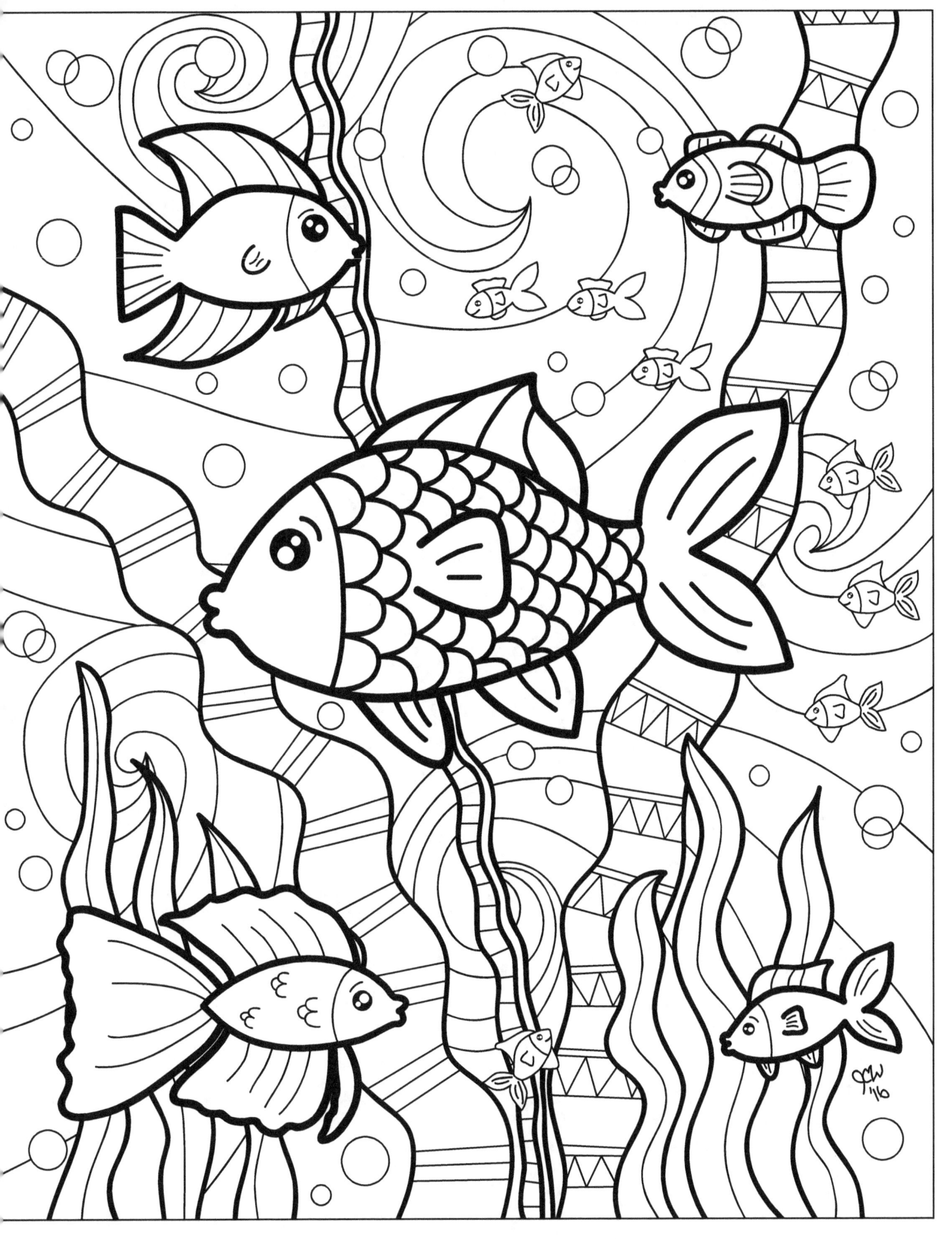

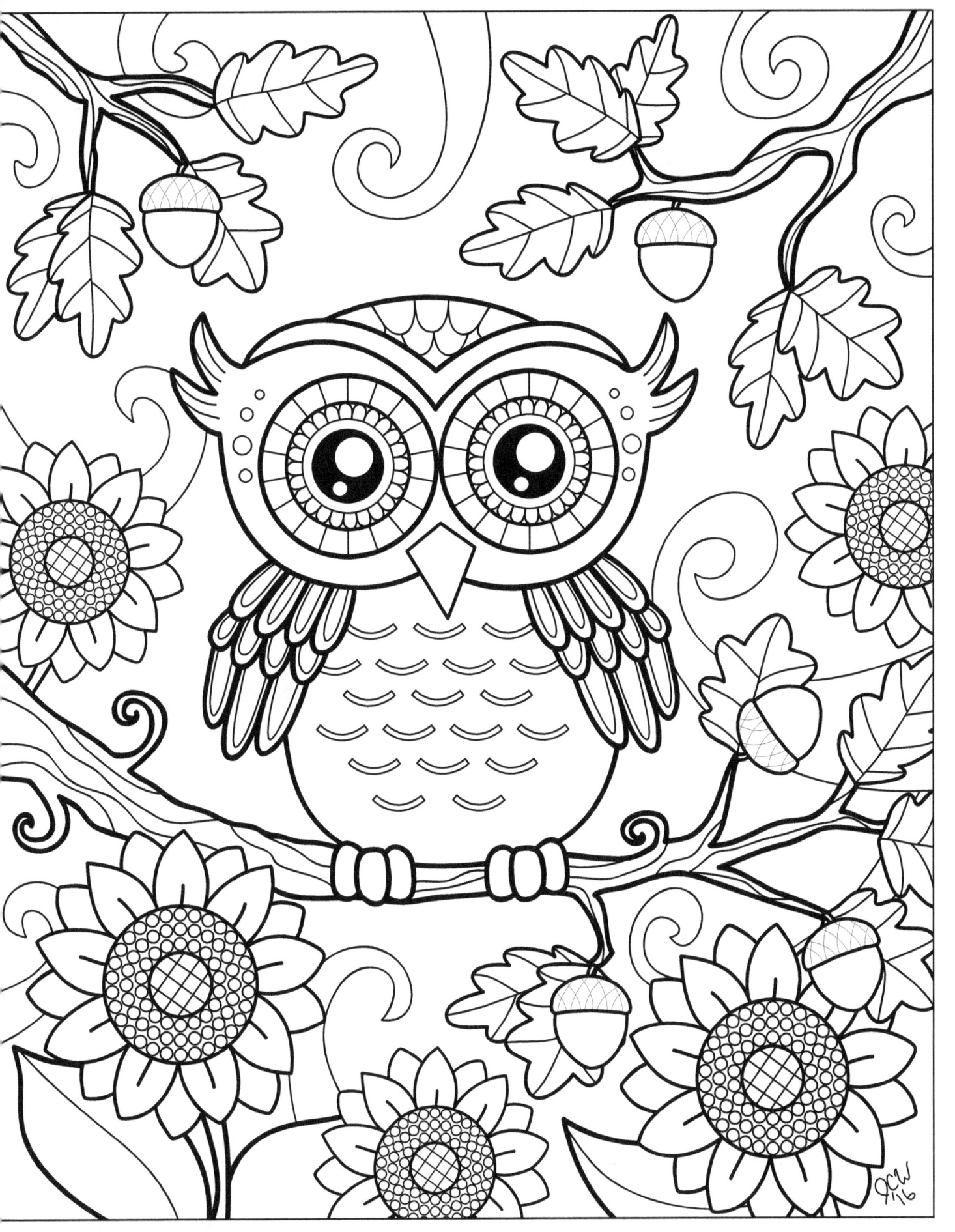

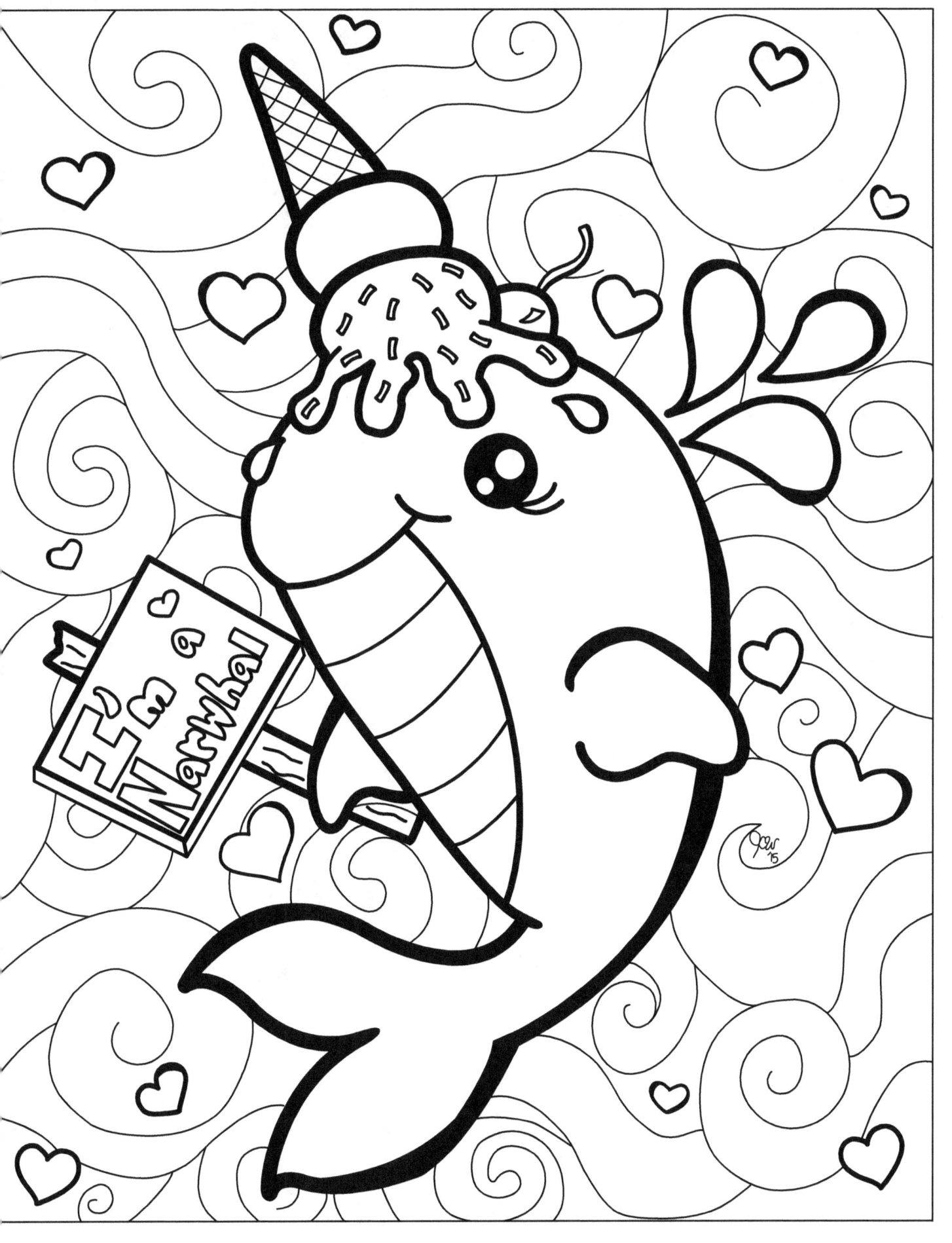

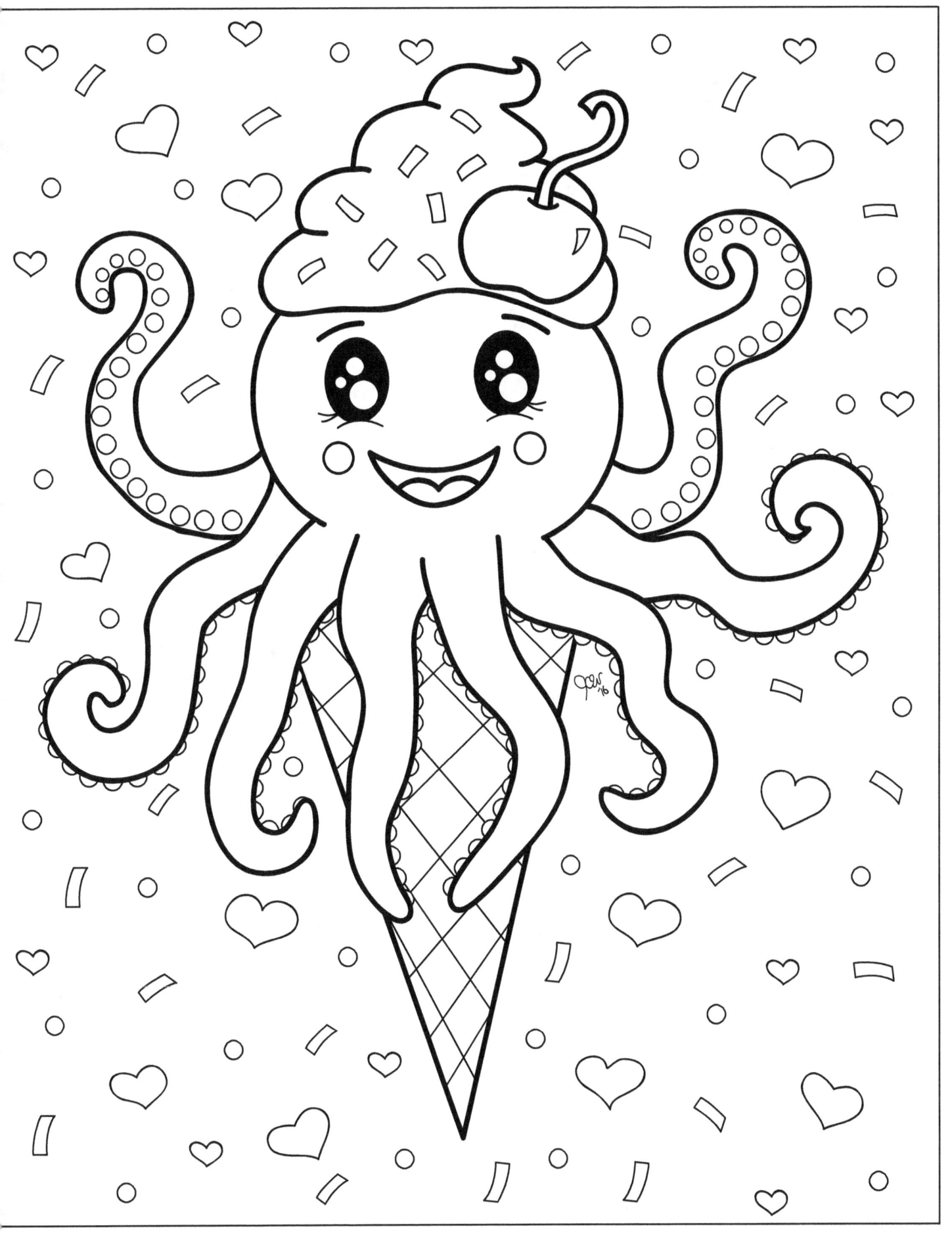

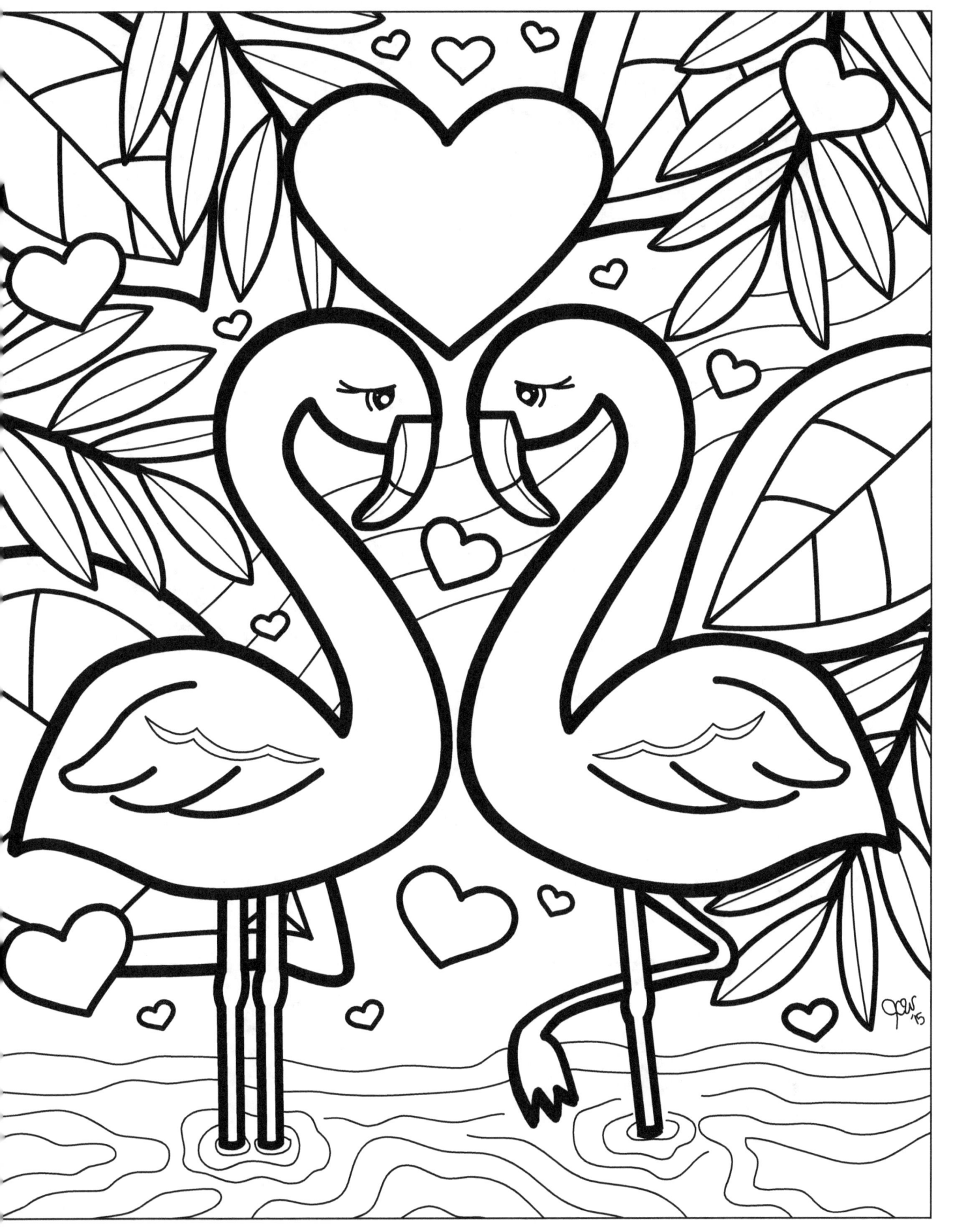

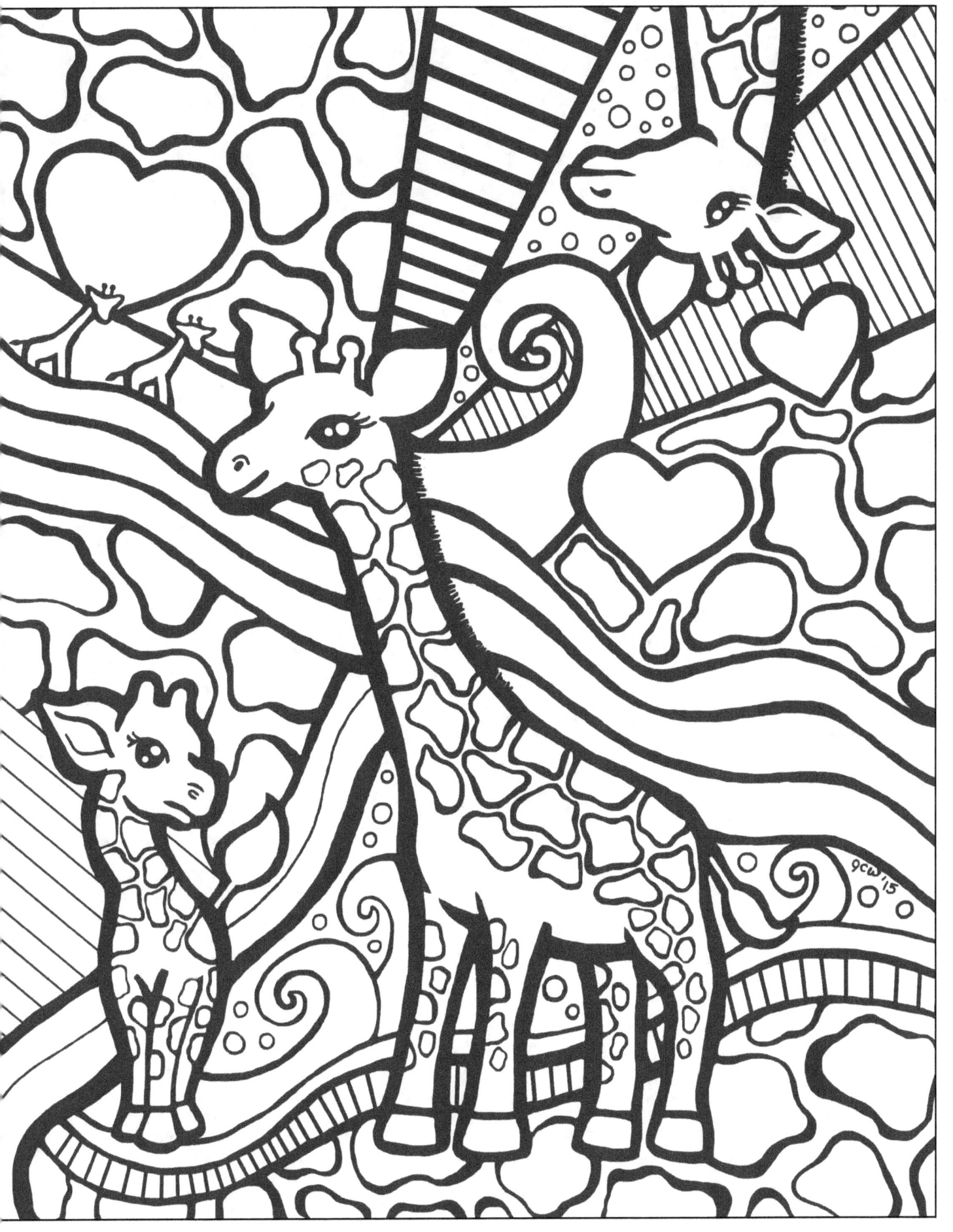

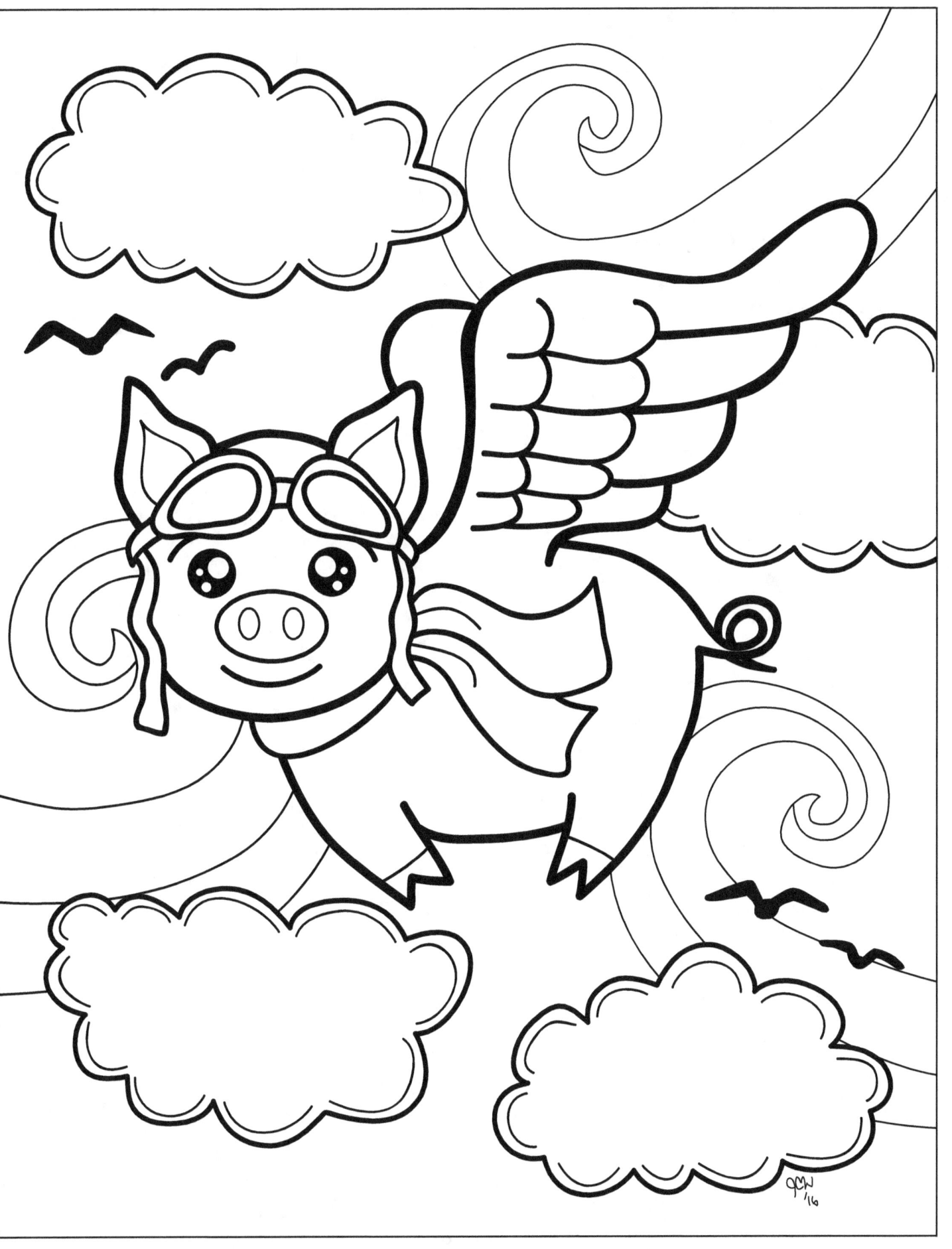

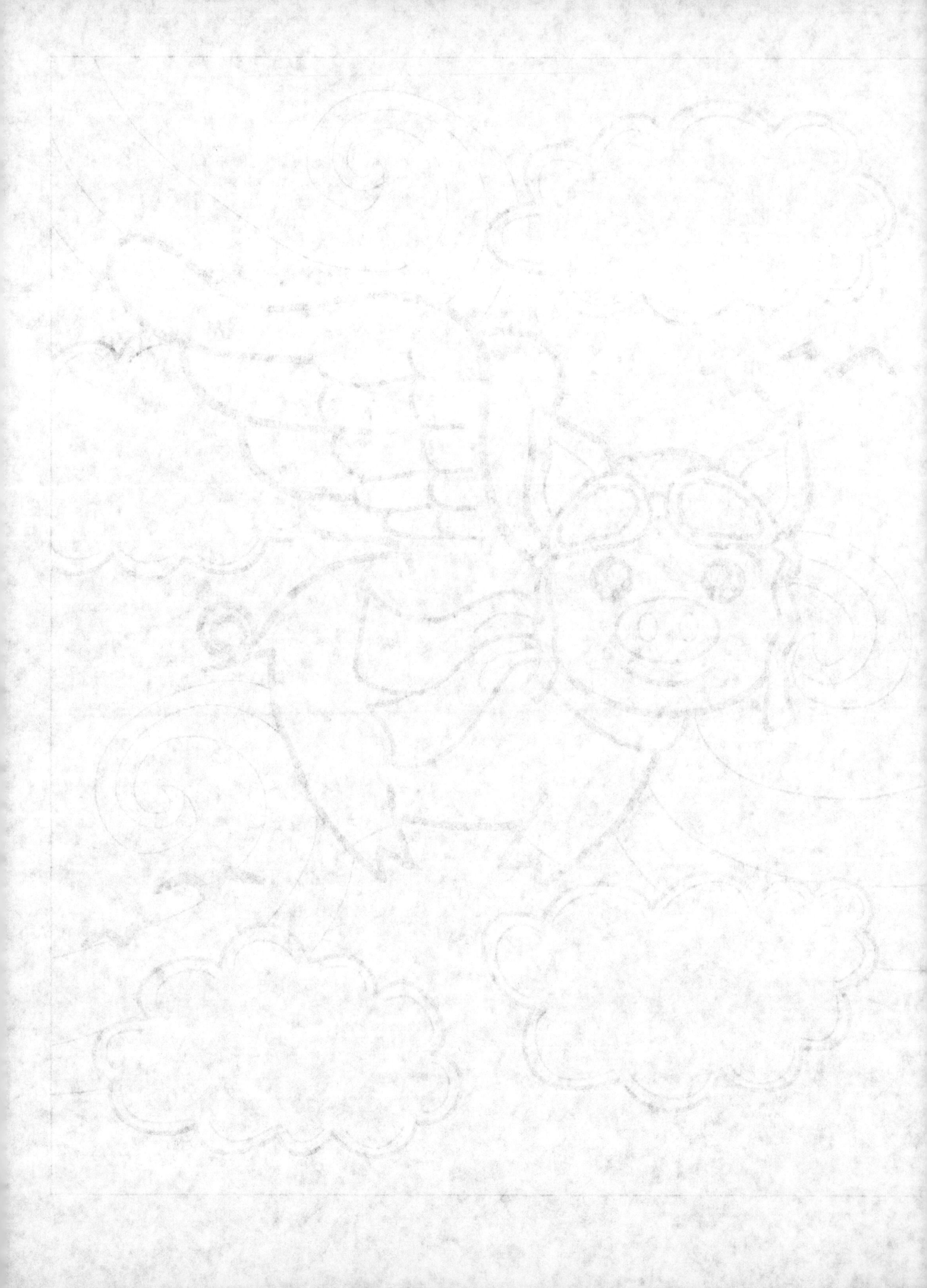

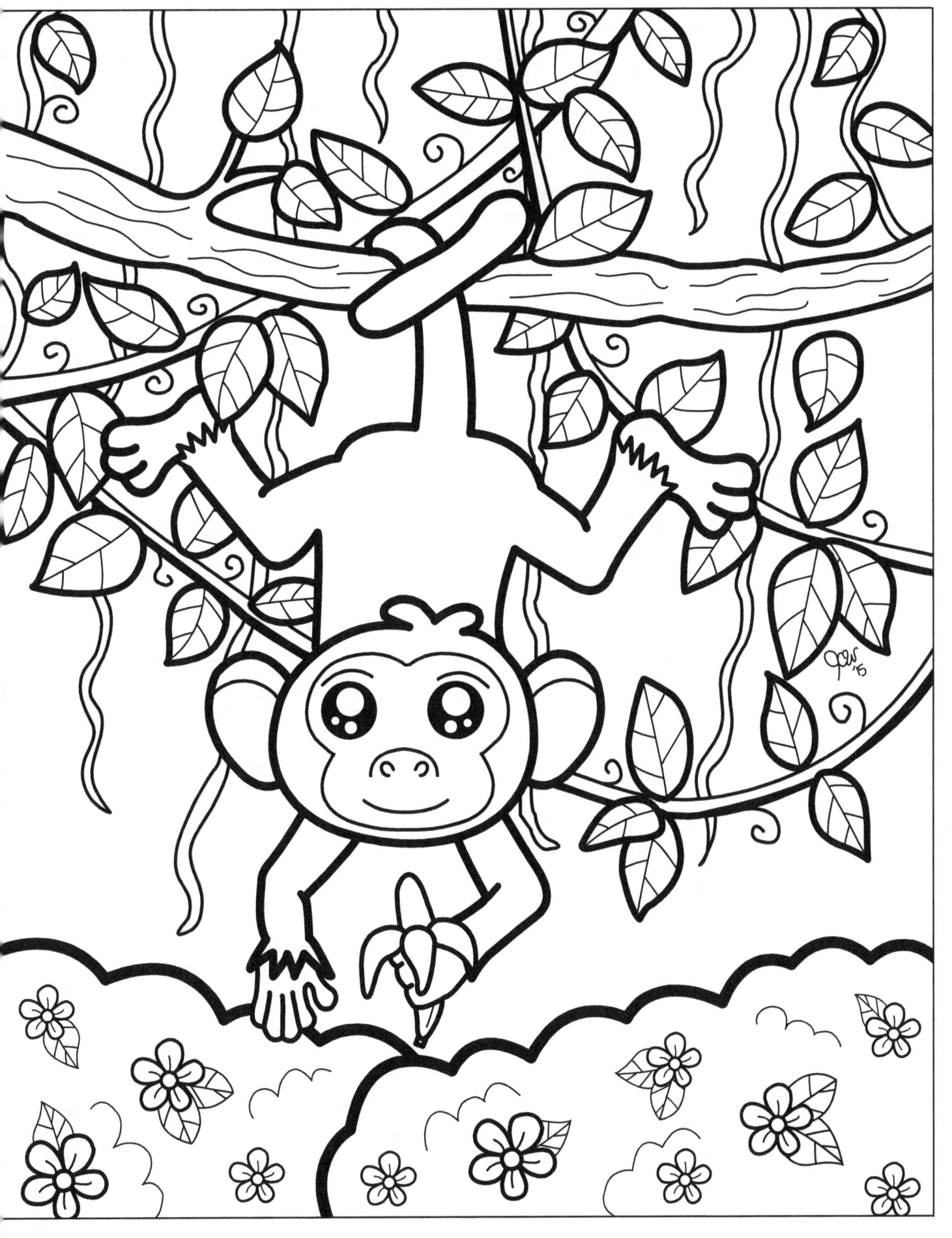

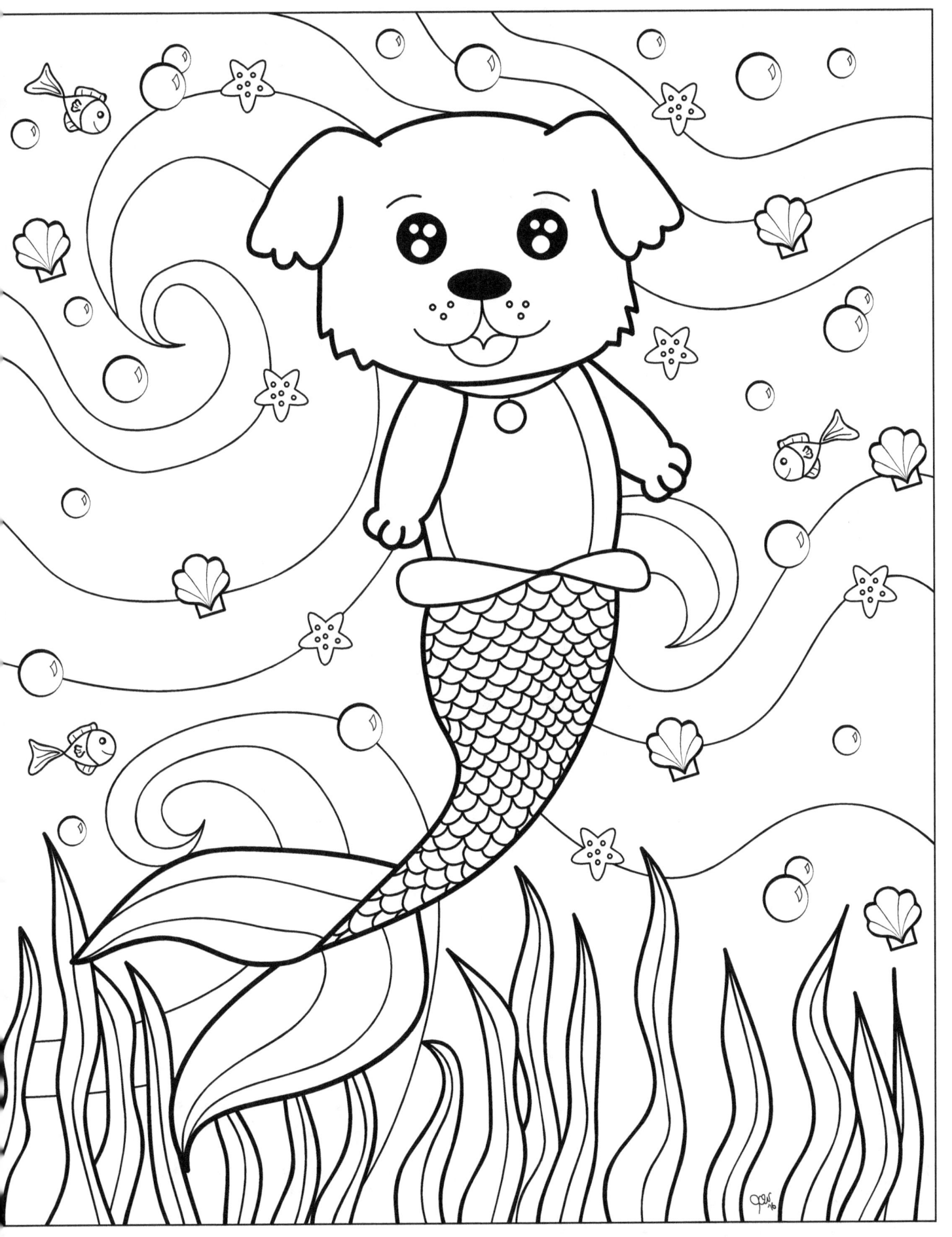

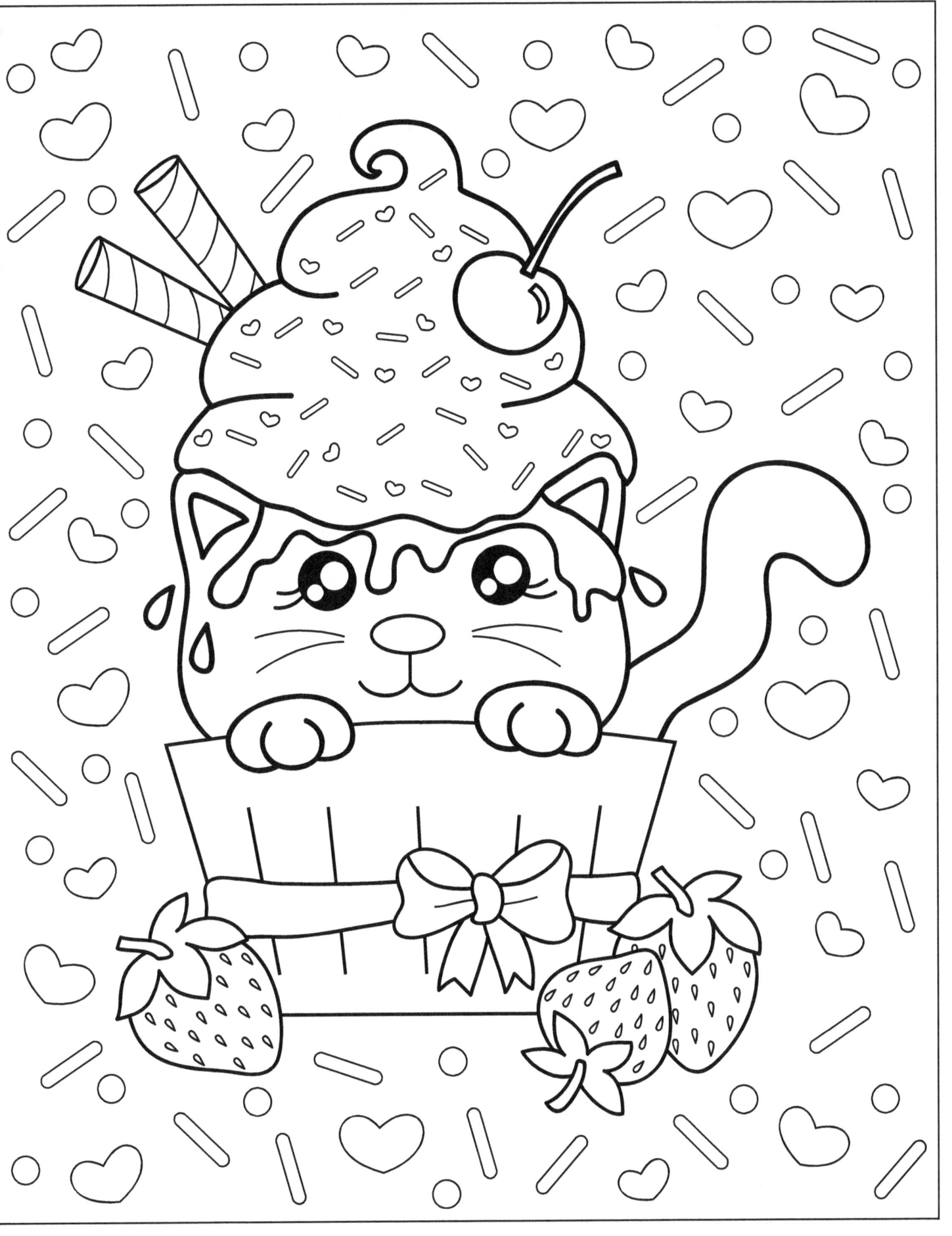

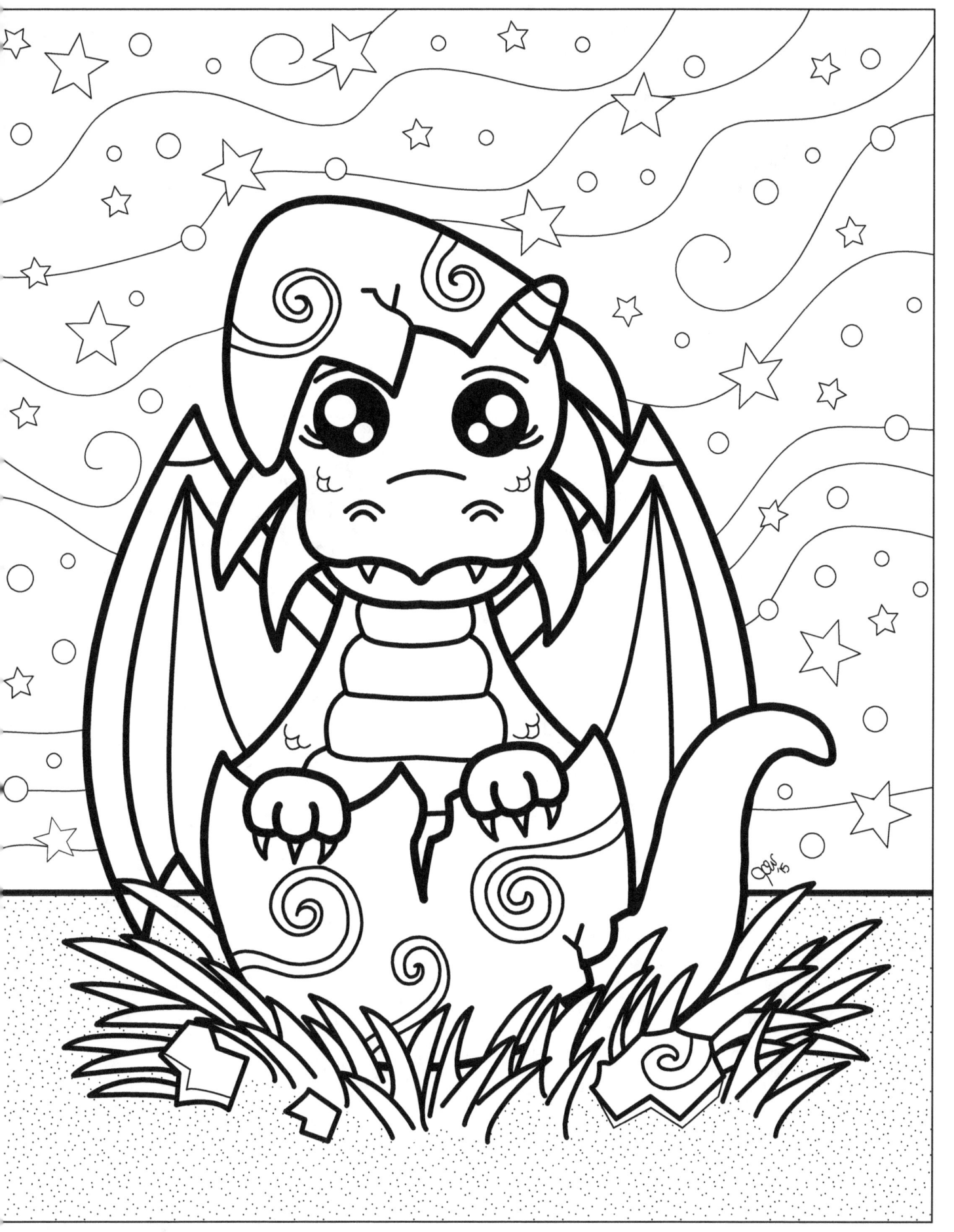

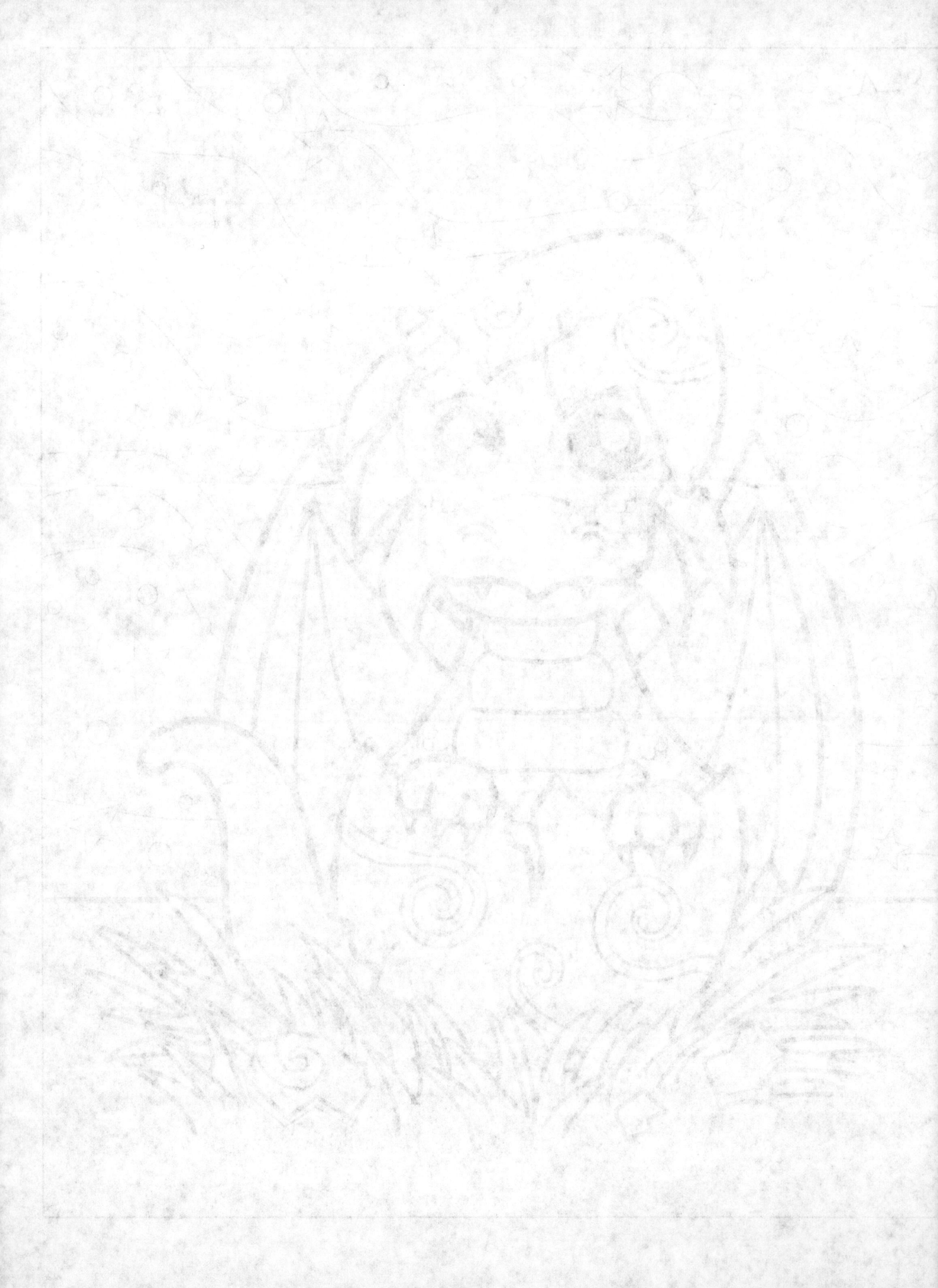

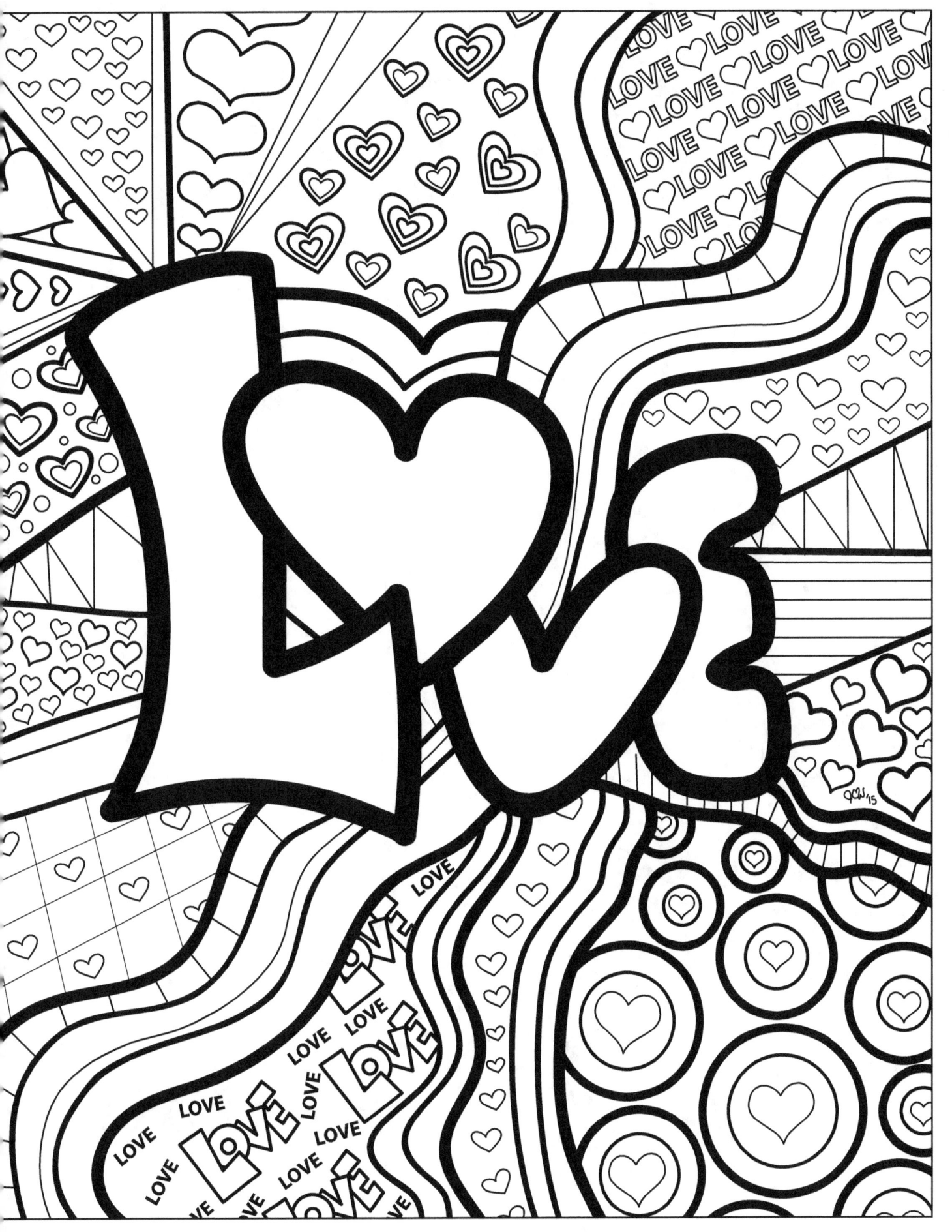

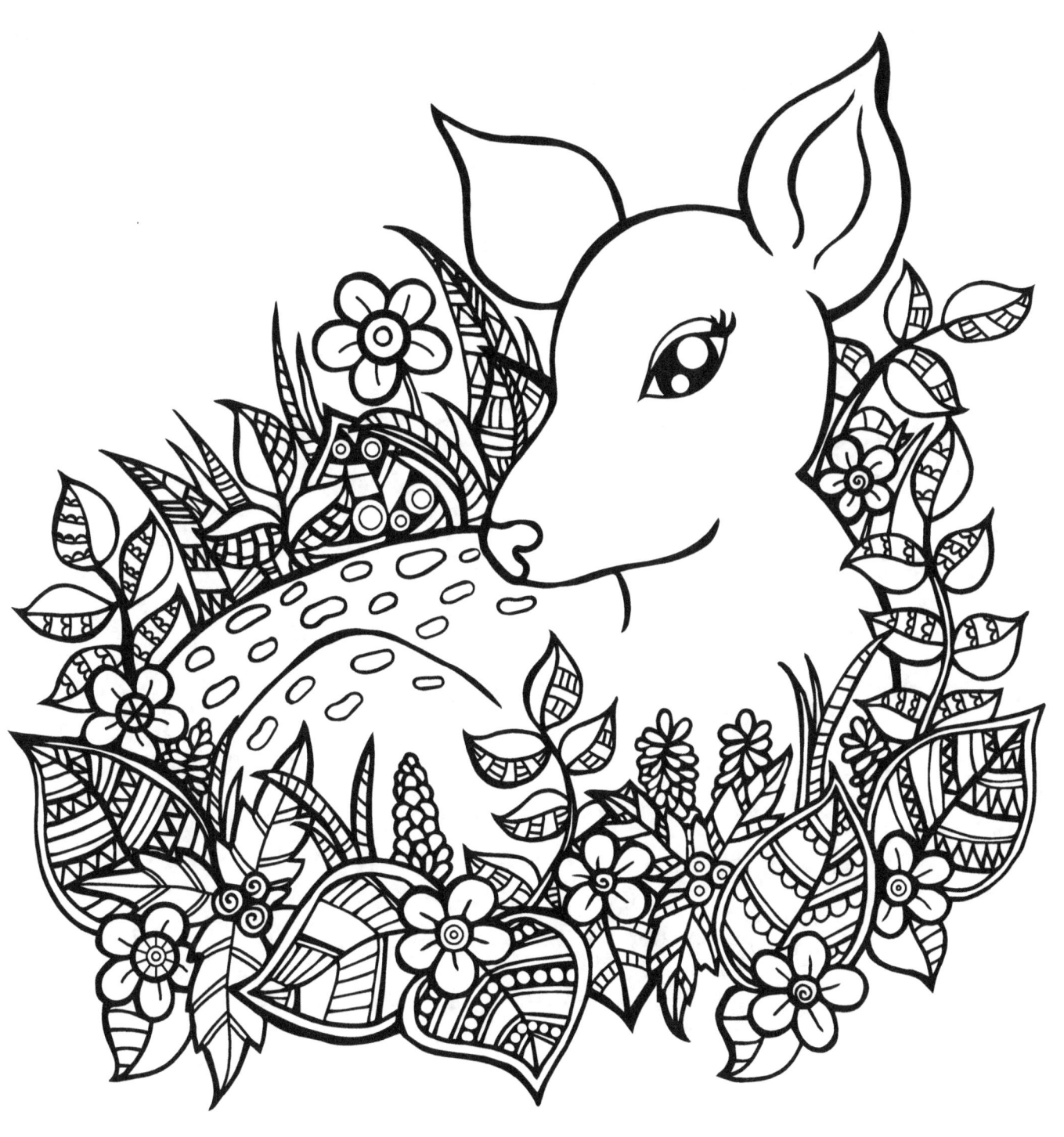

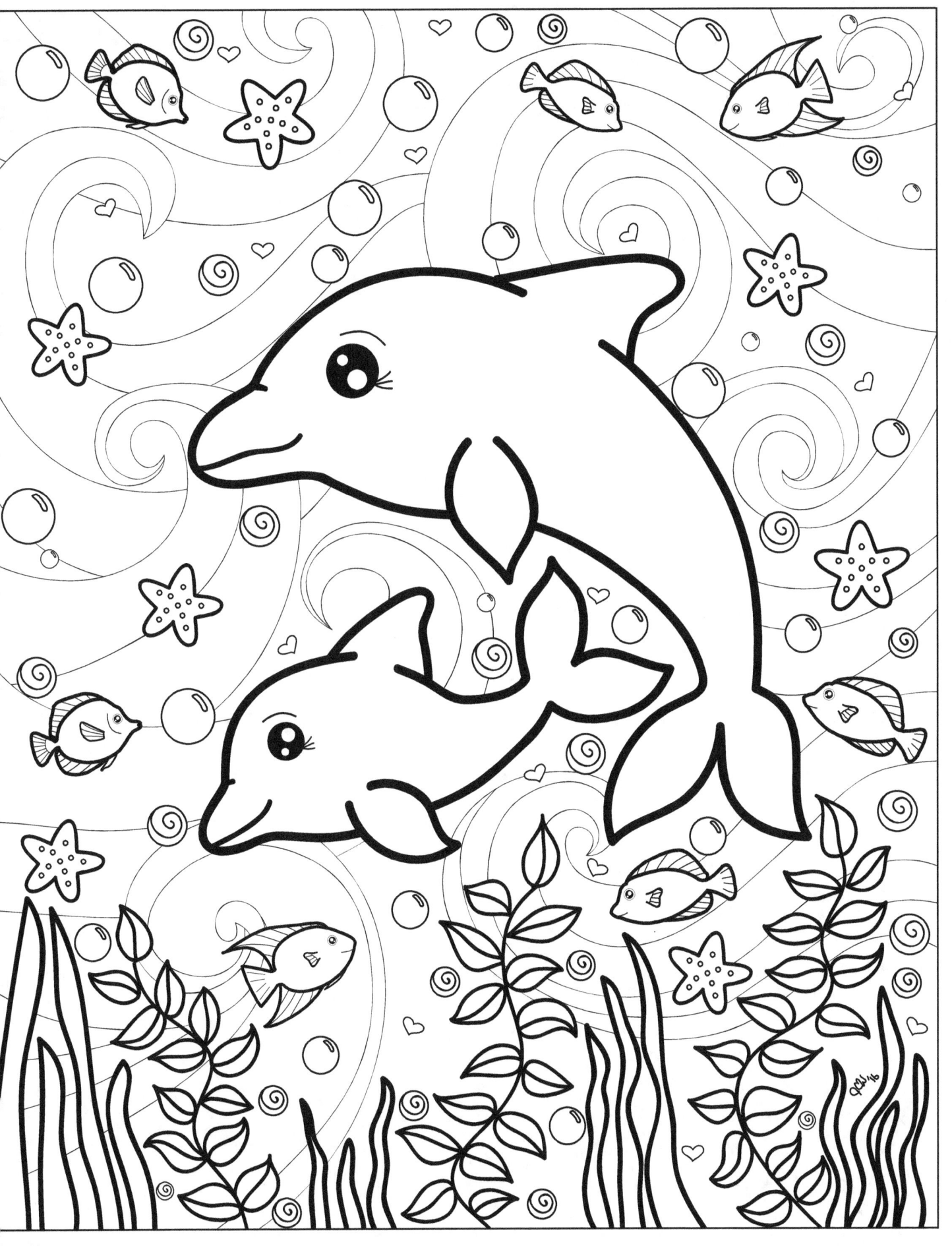

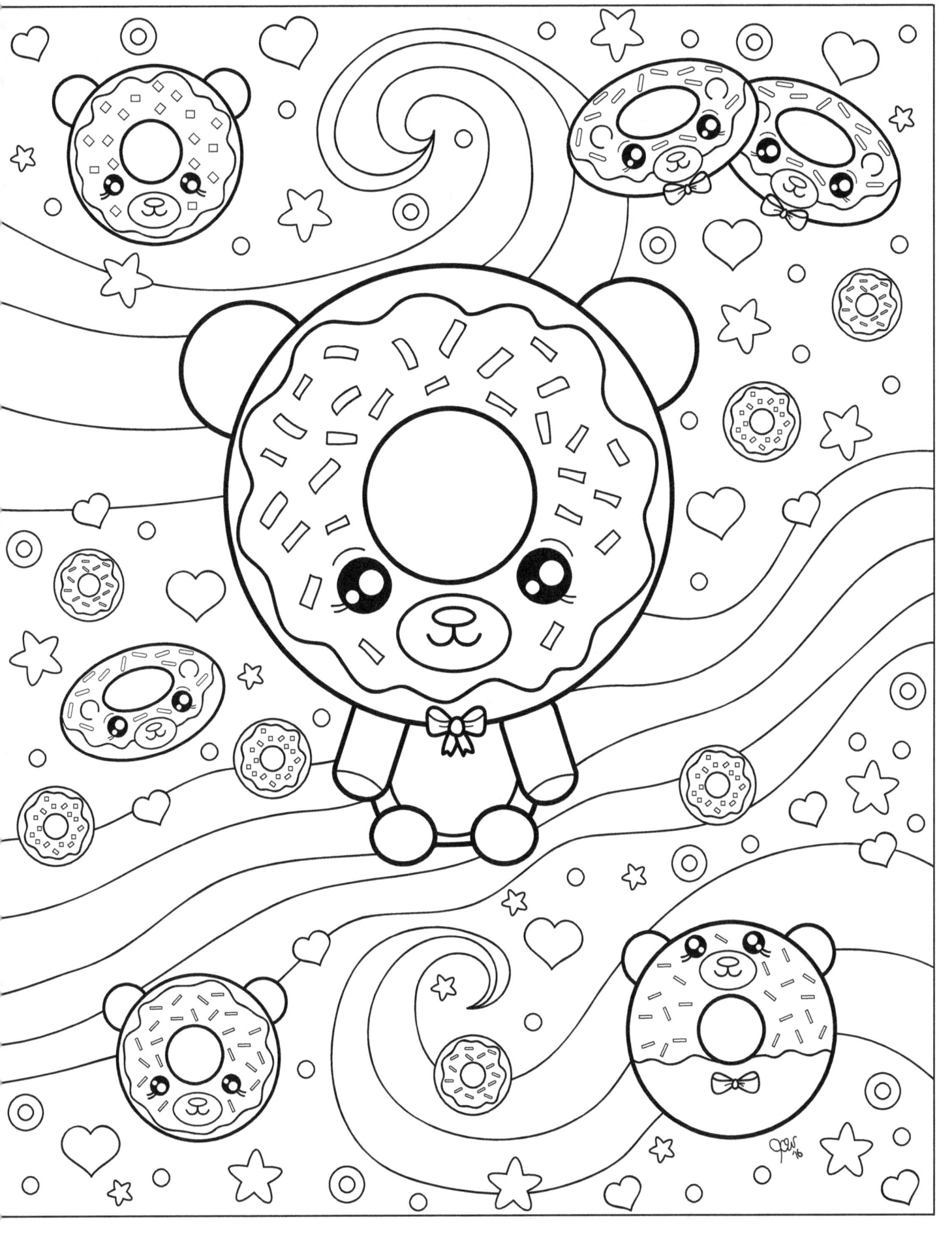

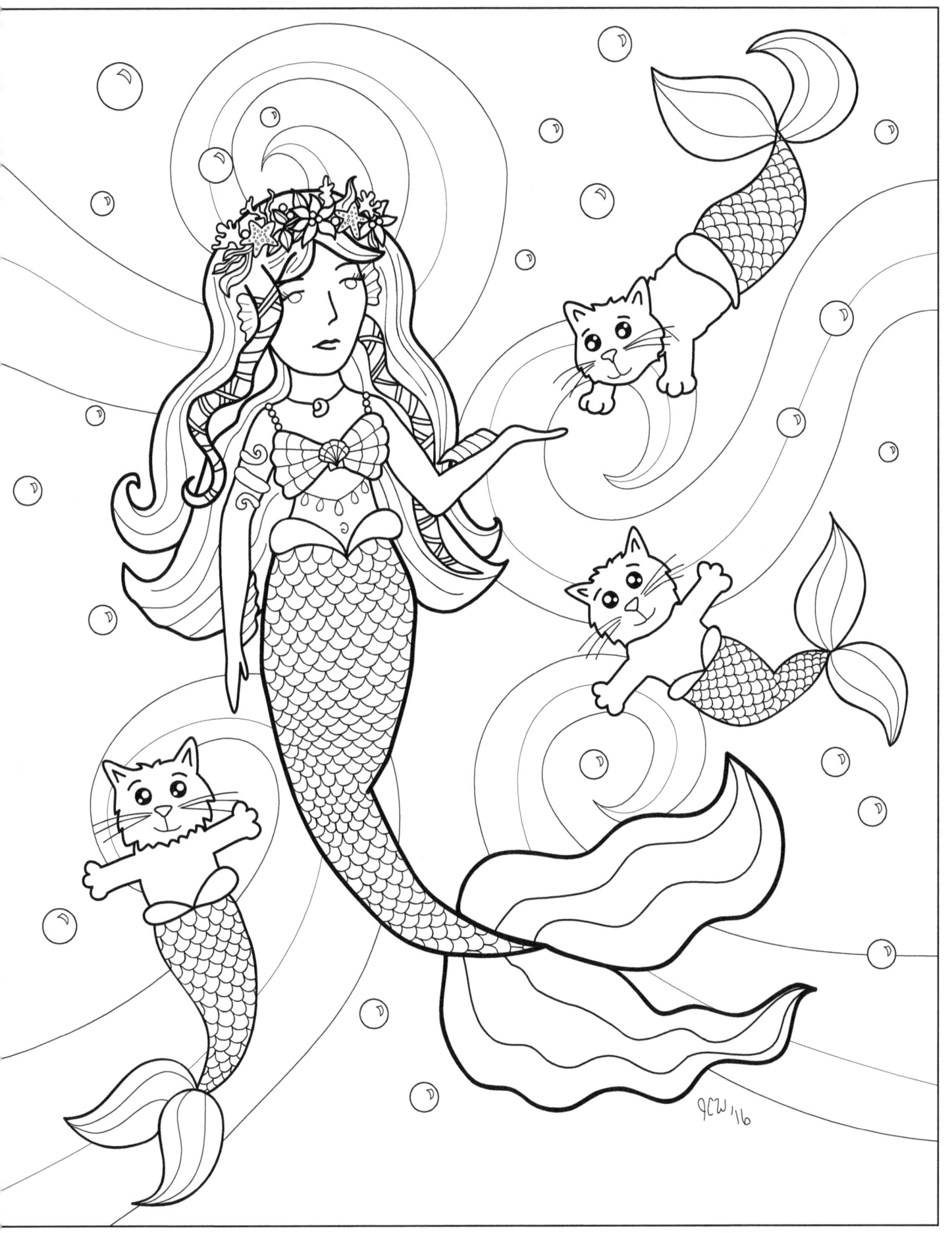

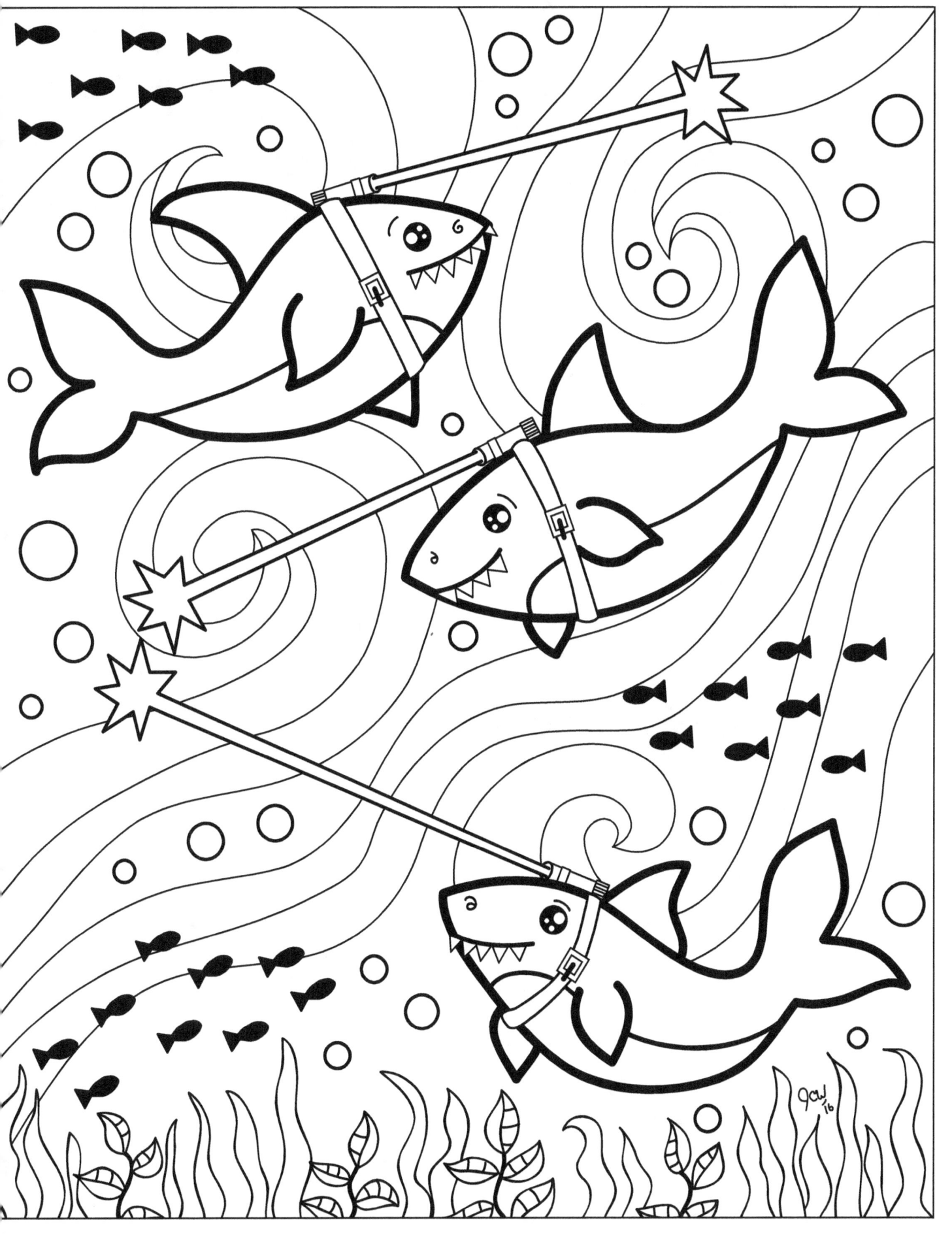

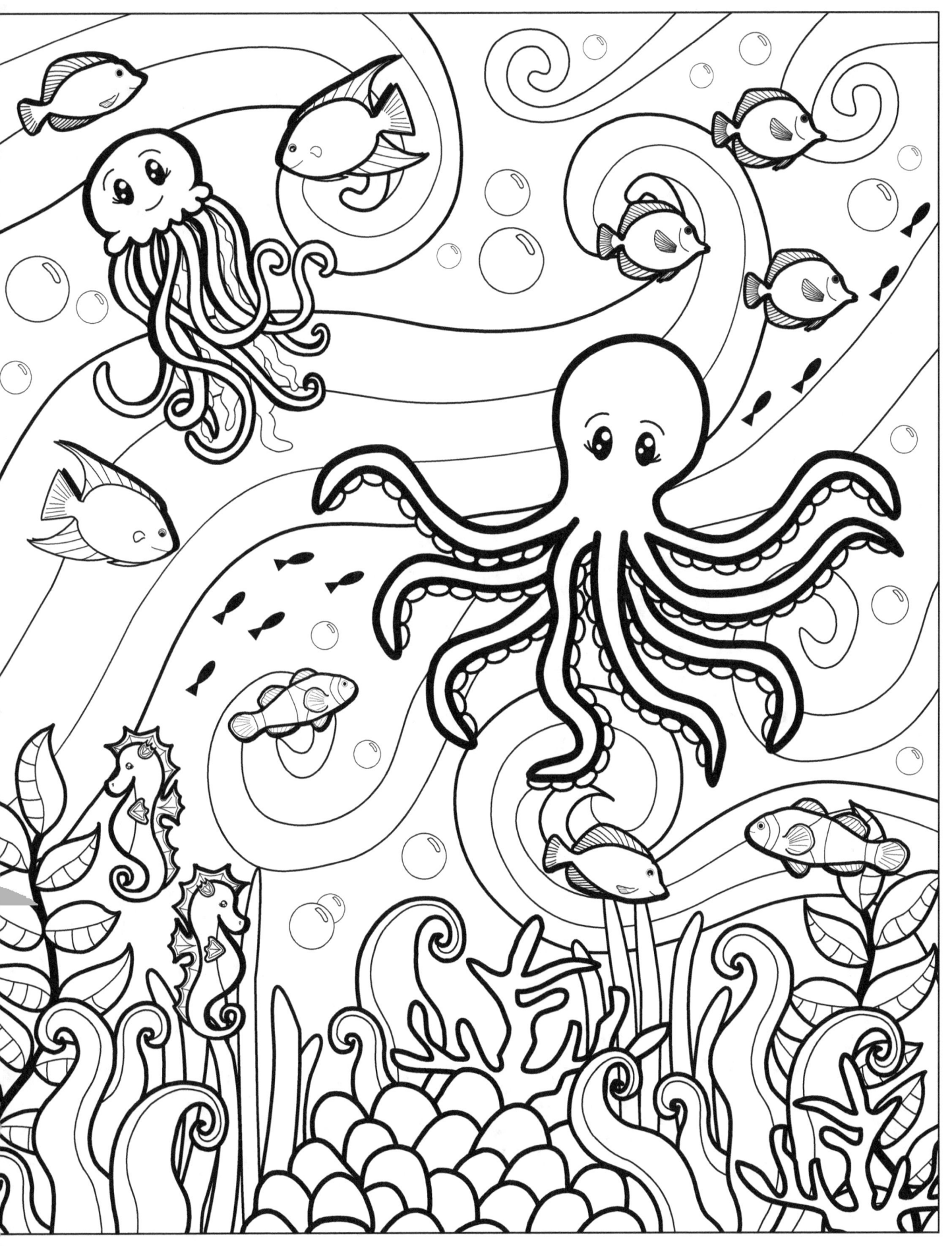

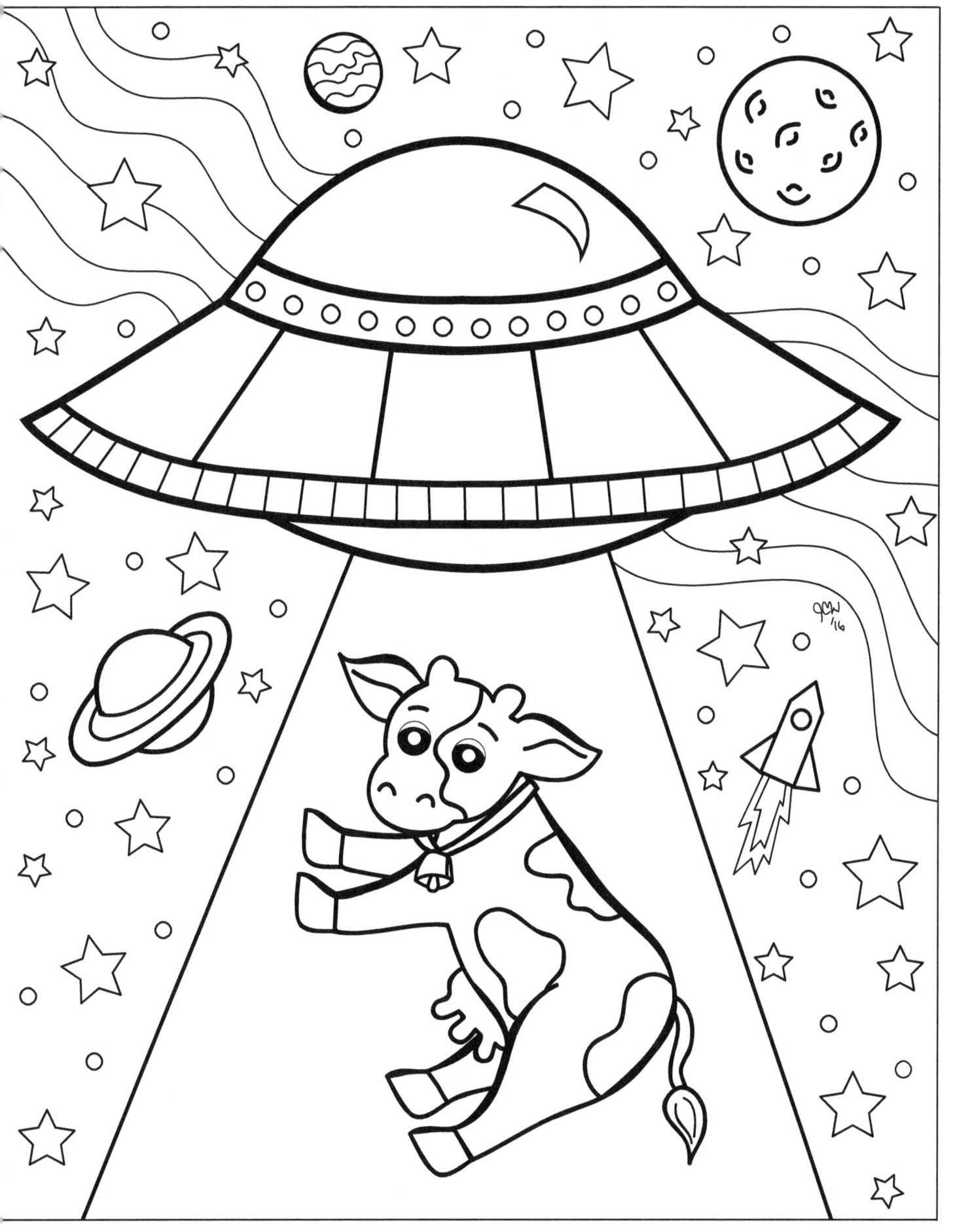

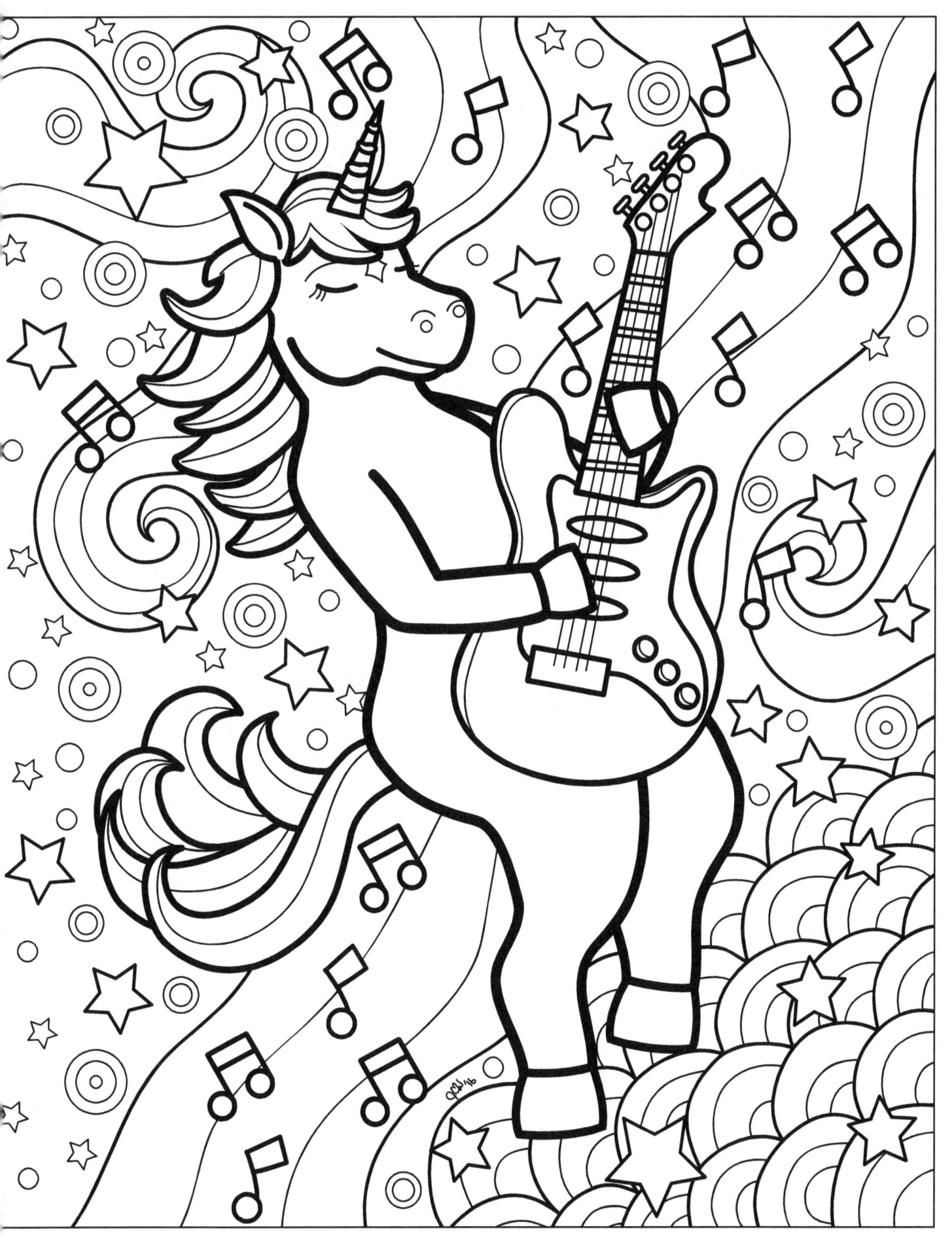

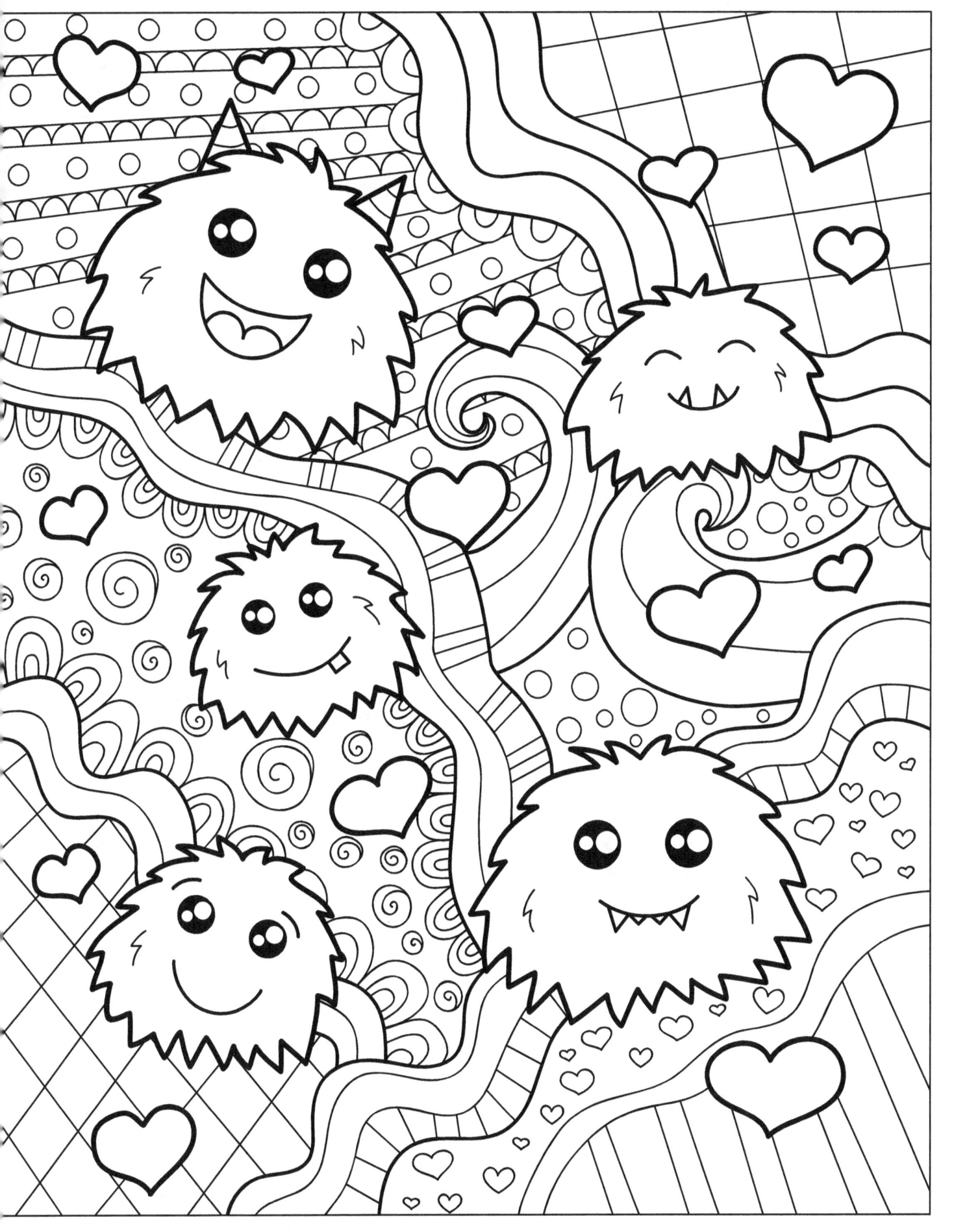

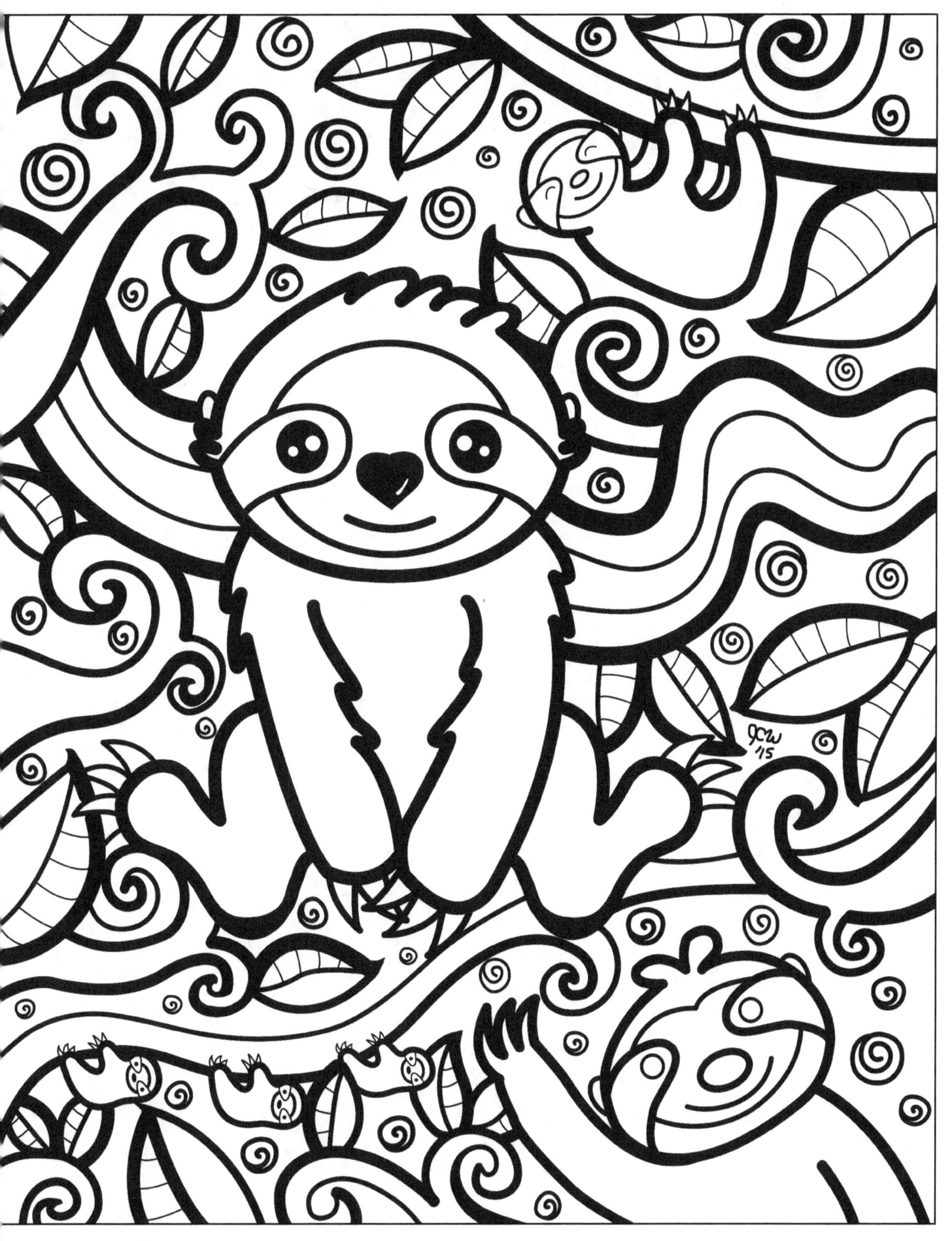

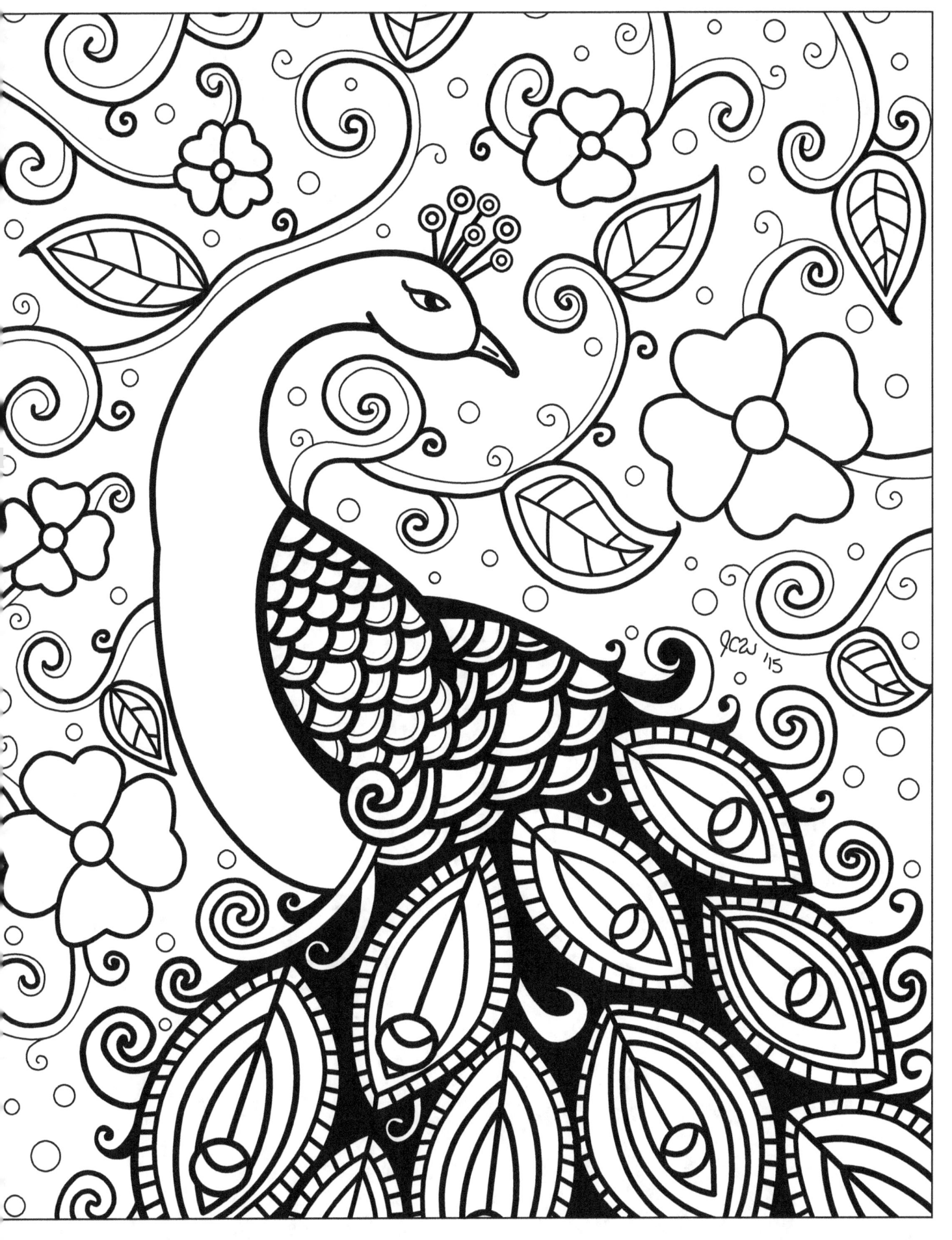

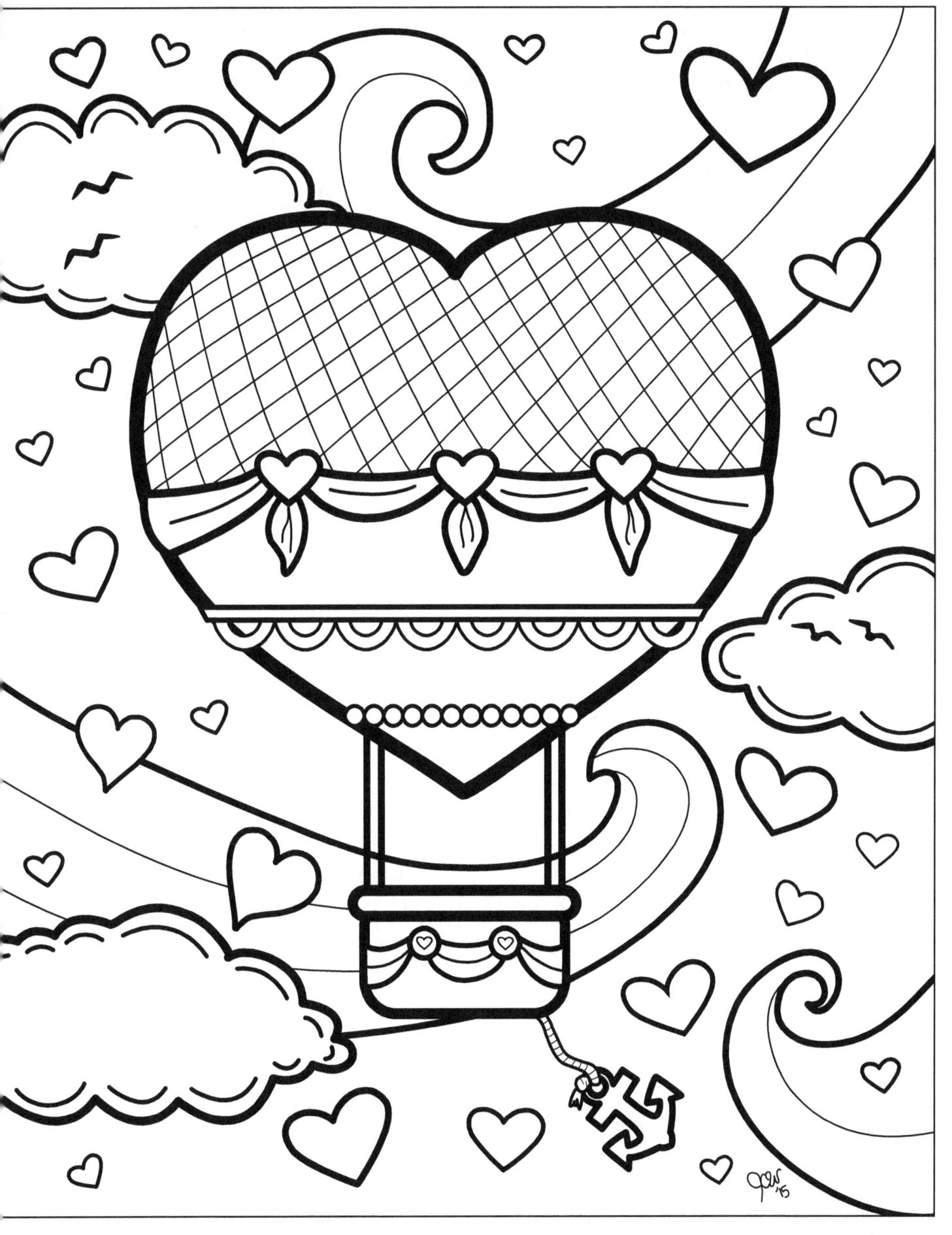

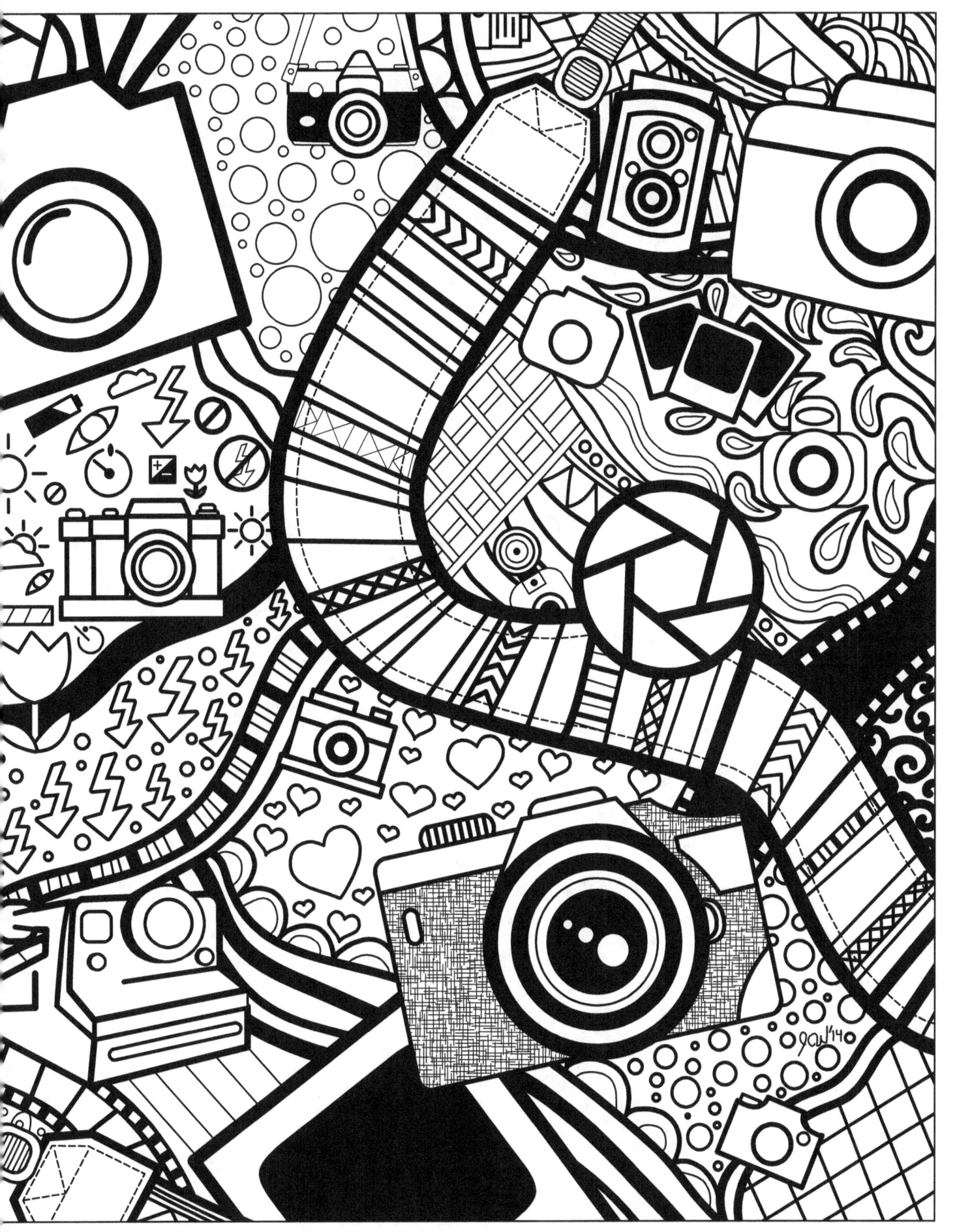

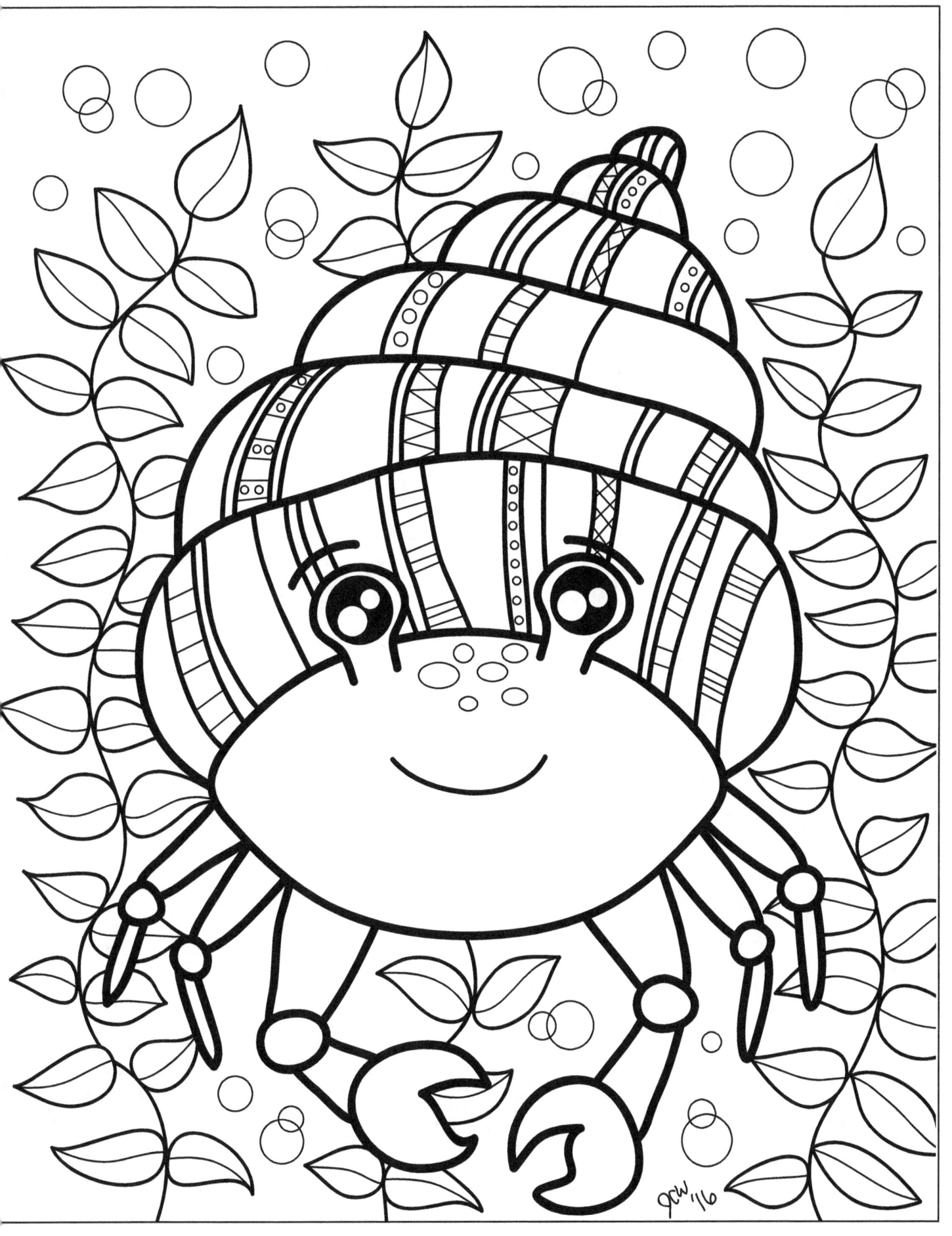

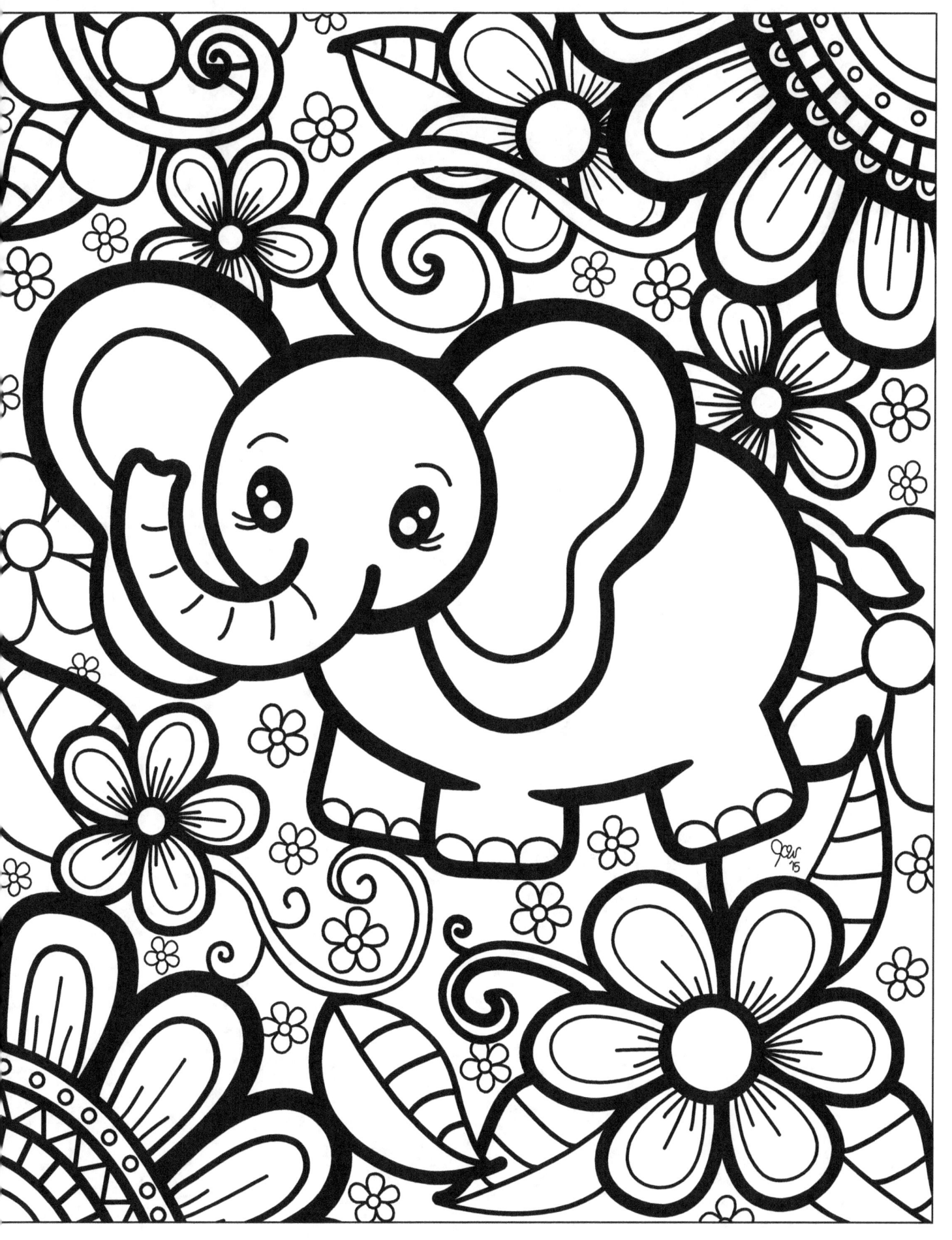

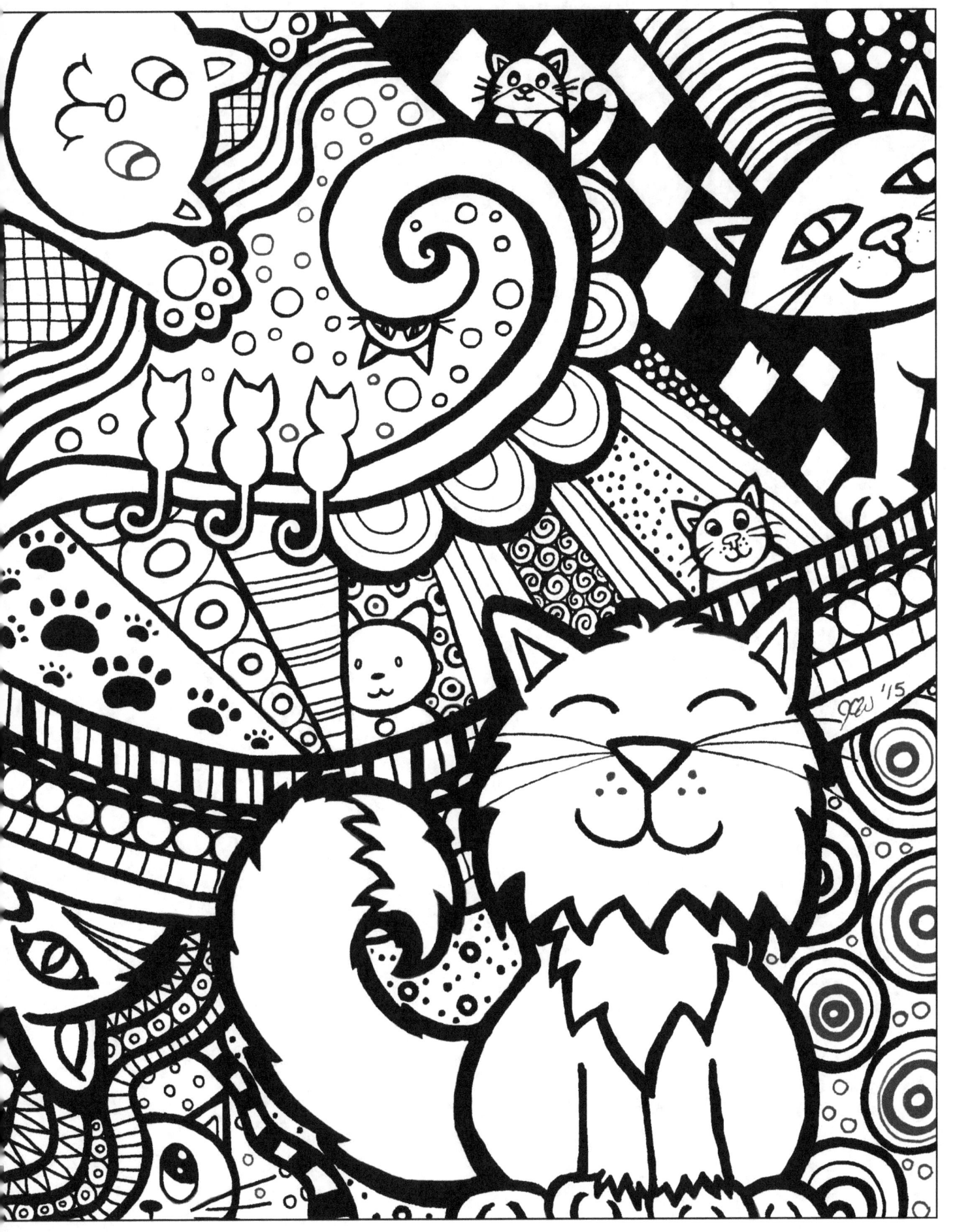

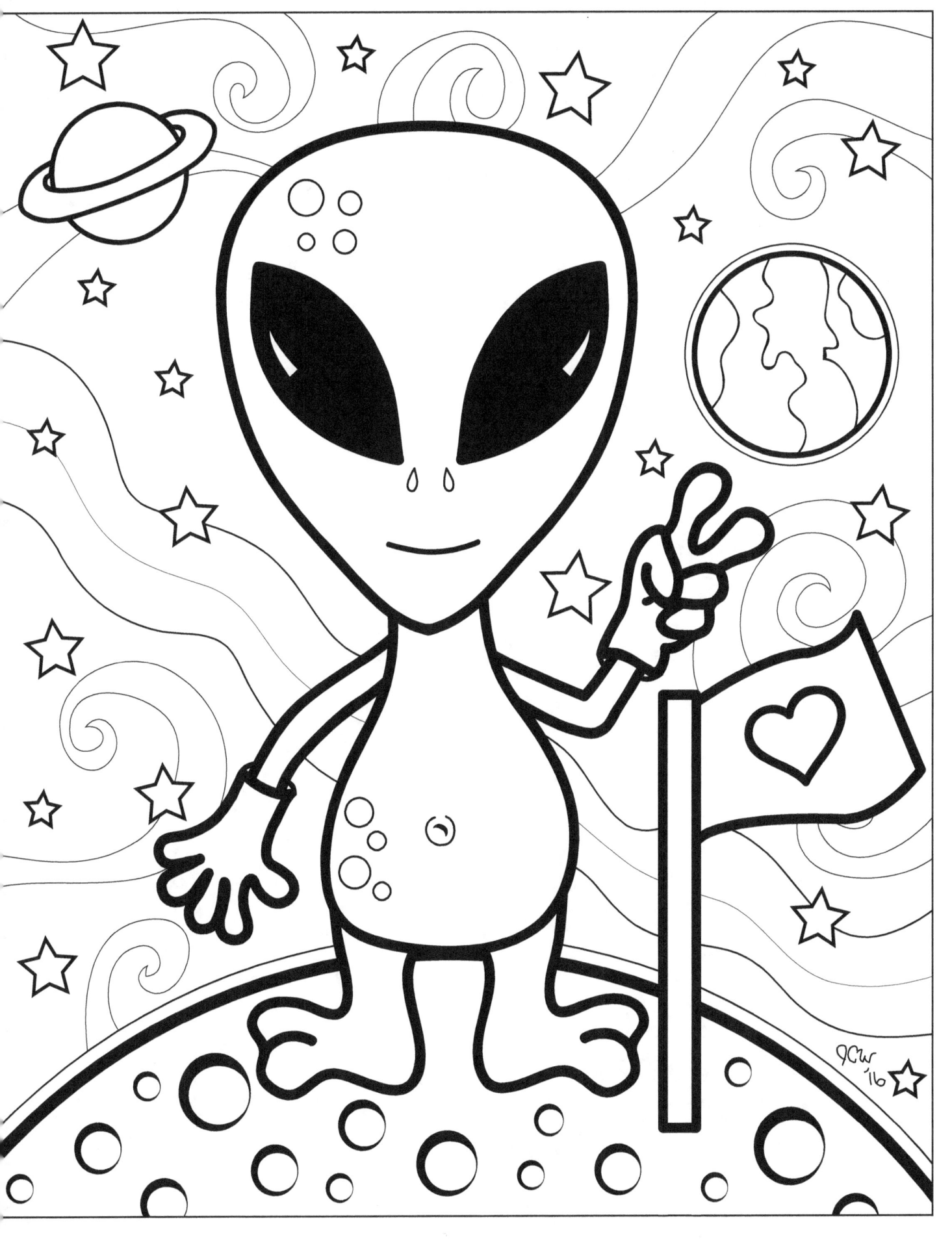

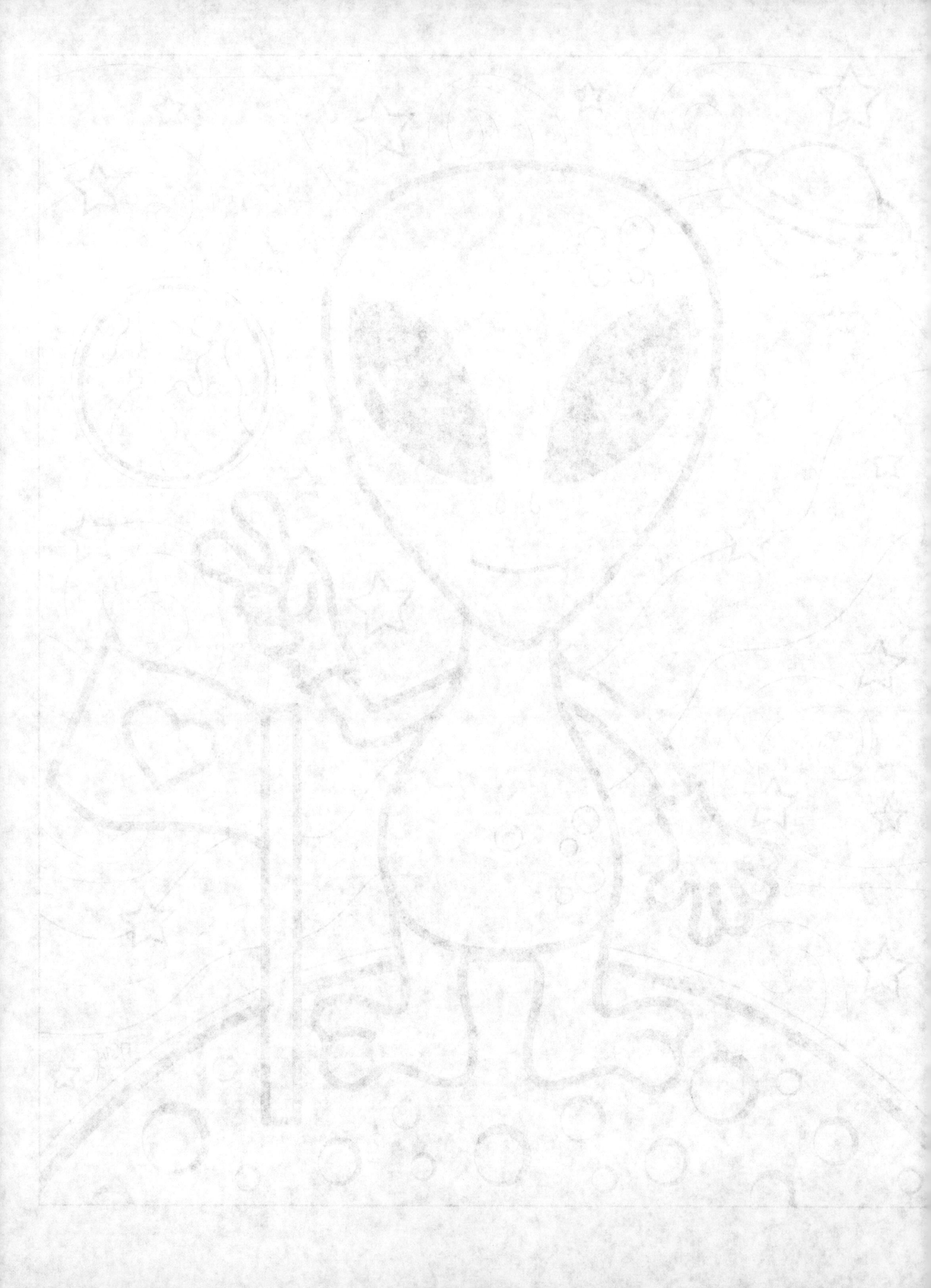

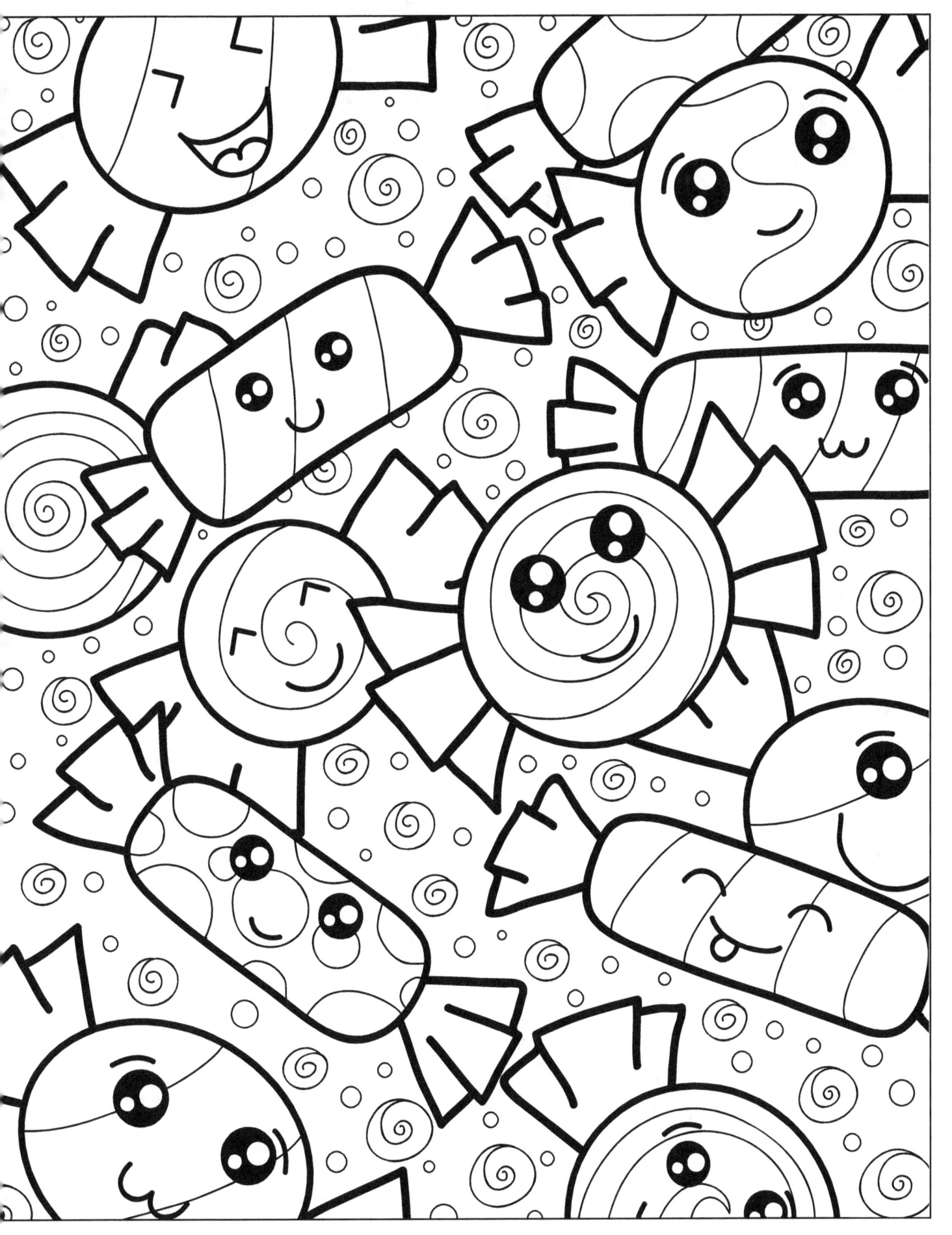